The Gorgon's Guide

Also by Laura Tempest Zakroff:

The New Aradia:
A Witch's Handbook to Magical Resistance
(Revelore Press, 2018)

Sigil Witchery:
A Witch's Guide to Crafting Magick Symbols
(Llewellyn, 2018)

Weave the Liminal:
Living Modern Traditional Witchcraft
(Llewellyn, 2019)

Anatomy of a Witch:
A Map to the Magical Body
(Llewellyn, 2021)

Visual Alchemy:
A Witch's Guide to Sigils, Art, & Magic
(Llewellyn, 2022)

The Gorgon's Guide
to Magical Resistance

Edited by
Laura Tempest Zakroff

Revelore Press
Olympia, WA
2022

The Gorgon's Guide to Magical Resistance

© REVELORE PRESS 2022.
All contributors retain copyright to their individual works.

All rights reserved. No part of this publication may be reproduced or utilized in any form or by any means, electronic or mechanical, including photocopying, recording, or by any information storage and retrieval system, without permission in writing from the Publishers.

The authors and publisher assume no responsibility for any errors or omissions. This book is not intended as a substitute for medical advice. No liability is assumed for damages that may result from the use of information contained within.

Book and cover design by Jenn Zahrt.
Cover image and illustrations by Laura Tempest Zakroff, unless otherwise noted.

ISBN PAPERBACK: 978-1-947544-43-7 EBOOK: 978-1-947544-45-1
Printed globally on demand through IngramSpark

First printed by REVELORE PRESS in 2022

REVELORE PRESS
1910 4TH AVE E PMB#141
Olympia, WA 98506
USA

www.revelore.press

The Gorgon's Guide to Magical Resistance

Contents

Introduction ~ 9
 Laura Tempest Zakroff

Martyrdom is the Last Resort ~ 11
 Alicia Vervain

The Offering to Persephone Praxidik ~ 15
 Terrance Gamble

Invoking the Ancestors of Revolution
A Spell to Support Your Radical Dreams & Actions ~ 18
 Lex Ritchie

Servitradis: A Servitor for Warning of Physical Danger ~ 21
 The Order of the Gorgon Shield

Bringing Sun to Earth:
A Tetrad++ic Protective Amulet ~ 23
 P. Sufenas Virius Lupus

Consecrating a Protective Charm to the Gorgons and Hekate ~ 27
 River Enodian

The Quartz Pentacle: A Spiritual Tool to
Sustain the Work of Restoring the World ~ 33
 Enrique Gomez

Political Money Magic ~ 37
 Star Bustamonte

The Reproductive Rights Sigil ~ 40
 Laura Tempest Zakroff

The Gorgon's Guide

Tongues, Vulvas, and Open Eyes:
Apotropaic Magic Against Patriarchy ~ 41
   Rev. Christian Ortíz

The Rite of Abominations:
A Sacrament of Sacred Termination ~ 45
   Georgia van Raalte

The Phallus Tree: An Historical Artifact
and a Contemporary Inspiration ~ 49
   Cory Thomas Hutcheson

Everyday Hexes and the Publicly Contested Body,
or, How to Get Clean to Do the Dirty Work ~ 52
   Jessica Della Janare

Hail to the Women ~ 55
   Heka deAuset

To Curse in the Name of Nemesis ~ 58
   Sara Mastros

Uerymurc: A Servitor for Undermining
Harmful Communication ~ 62
   The Order of the Gorgon Shield

A Thought-Form for Disruption ~ 65
   Philip Kane

Masks of Our Time ~ 69
   K.A.H

Heedless and Headless: The Witchcraft of Laverna ~ 73
   Thumper Forge

to Magical Resistance

The Apotropaic Power of Medusa's Blood:
Red Coral Charm to Ward Off Evil ~ 76
 Emiliano Russo

Transforming Anger Sigil ~ 79
 Laura Tempest Zakroff

Magick of/for the Fierce Hearts ~ 80
 Irisanya Moon

Cycle Breaker Sigil ~ 82
 Sidney Eileen

To Bind the Cruel ~ 85
 Ivy Senna

Boldly Reclaiming "I am" ~ 88
 Nova Pax Thrasher

Shadow Work with Snake Energy:
The Gorgon's Mask, Shame, and Self-Empowerment ~ 92
 Joey Morris

Flower Essences for Spiritual Activation ~ 96
 Lindsey Pszwaro

A Sigil for the Protection of Transgender Rights ~ 99
 Laura Tempest Zakroff

A Sigil to Defend Transfolx ~ 100
 Laura Tempest Zakroff

Invocation of the Outlander ~ 101
 M. Belanger

The Gorgon's Guide

Opening Hearts Ritual ~ 103
    Fr. Sean Wilde UE

Citadel of Stone, Roots, and Ivy ~ 106
    Gwynevere Kipling

Deep Green Witchcraft and the Spirits of Place ~ 109
    Dodie Graham McKay

Three Workings for Protection ~ 113
    Estara Sanatani

Reclaiming Power: An Apple Charm ~ 116
    M. Belanger

Separation and Recuperation Spell ~ 119
    Rev. Laura González

Strength in Stillness ~ 121
    The Weavers

ACKNOWLEDGEMENTS ~ 124
CONTRIBUTORS ~ 125
RESOURCES ~ 133

to Magical Resistance

Introduction

IN FALL OF 2018 – JUST AHEAD OF THE US ELECTIONS, the *New Aradia: A Witch's Handbook to Magical Resistance* was released. Created as a collection of ideas to teach, share, inspire, empower, protect, and guide, found within its pages are sigils, spells, recipes, essays, invocations, rituals, and more - all gathered from experienced magical practitioners from around the world. In addition to being a reference guide, a portion of sales from the *New Aradia* benefited the Southern Poverty Law Center and Emily's List (over $3500 collectively as of Fall 2022.)

While change is afoot, we continue to exist in a timeline rife with conflict and crisis. The need for another collection to help address the changing landscape has become clearly evident. And so *The Gorgon's Guide* has been called into being.

The Gorgon's Guide follows in the footsteps of the first volume of *New Aradia*, digging deeper into magical work that is relevant to our times. Magical resistance happens both through physical means and metaphysical works—mind, body, and spirit. We seek not only to survive, but to thrive and craft new possibilities for tomorrow—for humanity, for the planet, for all. For this edition, we have worked to center the voices of queer, trans, and BIPOC practitioners and related issues as much as possible.

And like *New Aradia*'s proven financial commitment to ushering change, with every purchase of this book, $1 will be sent to a national and a local non-profit organization, rotating on a quarterly basis. Our first two chosen groups are: Indigenous Women Rising (https://www.iwrising.org/) and Holler Health Justice (https://www.hollerhealthjustice.org/)

Why is this volume called Gorgon's Guide? Emerging from Greek mythology, the Gorgons are beings often described as having snakes

The Gorgon's Guide

in place of hair, large eyes, scaly skin, teeth like boars, claws for hands, and golden wings. They could petrify anyone who looked directly into their eyes. The number of Gorgons varies, but the most popular mythology describes the Gorgons as three sisters. Some say the Gorgons represent perversion in its three forms: Medusa (intellectual), Euryale (sexual) and Steno (moral). For centuries, witches have been said to be the perverse ones, upsetting the order of society. But what if society *needs* upsetting?

Right now, we are under attack: the truths of science and logic are being undermined; queer, trans, and reproductive rights are in grave danger; and the powers that be turn a blind eye to climate change, environmental destruction, and basic human rights. If fighting against these violations is perverse, then Gorgons we shall be.

We may not have snakes in our hair, but we hold the power of the Serpent within us. The primal voice within us, the Serpent speaks of creation and change, power and protection, venom and vision. It reminds us that the path of living is serpentine—in moving forward we must also be prepared to spiral back, as well as knowing when to rest and when to strike. The Serpent says to the Witch, "Kiss the air with your tongue, move your body like water, let your spirit burn like fire, and glide upon the earth with ease."

Remember the strength and power that resides within you, for you are a being of change, a child of Gorgons.

Laura Tempest Zakroff
Providence, RI
October 2022

to Magical Resistance

Martyrdom is the Last Resort

This anger is cold.
Empty. Hollow.
It is not the raging fire of a forest sparking
against the black sky.

It is that sky.
It is the ash and smoke and charred meat of bodies
that have more value
than the lives they inhabit,
whose wombs carry more potential
than they themselves could
ever aspire to,
whose inalienable rights
are oh so very fragile and alien
after all.

We see you.
With glassy eyes and burnt throats,
we curse your names,
you who dictate that which you do not have
and choose not to understand,
and those of you who do,
who have betrayed your own
only to be faced with the flames
yourselves.

We know you.

The Gorgon's Guide

May.
You.
Burn.

May your body
cease to heed your every
wish or whim or need.

May every bite of sustenance turn
to maggots and ash on your tongue.

May every joy you know
wither and decay in your hands
and at your feet
like a putrid, lonely Midas.

May your dreams be nothing
but mirrors and the sick sound of
gore rent from bone
and that endless
endless dark.

May you know cataclysm
and devastation
and Apocalypse.

And when you light that next match
already held in your filthy
creeping fingers,
may you find your own flesh
to be the kindling.

to Magical Resistance

We may be the monsters,
but you,
you who sit on your modern-day thrones
and make decisions that will never touch you,
you are the corrupt kings
who send your people
to die
knowing there are answers
less brutal.

So yes, I will brew teas of
cotton root bark and rue.
I'll make oil of pennyroyal
and crush the root of black cohosh with its kin.
I am good friends with Queen Anne
and there is already
blood on the lace.

I will break your laws and my own bones
if I must,
because I promise you,
I will remove my womb from this earth
before I let you rape and reap it for your
rotting
Garden of Eden.

I may be the monster.
But you're the ones who made me.
And I am less afraid of the fire
than you think.

The Gorgon's Guide

This anger
is cold
and empty.
There is an echo
where my birthright
used to be.

But you cannot pluck
Sovereignty
from a cold dead husk
that once housed
hope.

May you never
know peace
again.

Alicia Vervain
24th June 2022

to Magical Resistance

The Offering to Persephone Praxidike

Terrance Gamble

Praxidike is commonly known as the daimon of Justice. However, in the *Orphic Hymns* Praxidike was equated with the goddess Persephone. The title "Praxidike" means Exacter of Justice, indicating that this title or aspect of Persephone exacts justice not simply for the dead of her realm, but upon the Earth as well. In orphism, Persephone is mother to Zagreus-Dionysus and the Eumenides, or Kindly Ones, also known as the Furies. The Eumenides are also spirits of exacting justice, but specifically horrendous violent crimes against members of the family, the vulnerable within society and disrespect to customs governing hospitality.

Should you have experienced such grievances by the hand of an individual or institution this is an appropriate offering ritual to gain Praxidike's graces while her daughters exact justice. This is of course a ritual one may do on behalf of others, whether you know them personally or not. Compile a list of names to recite at the end of the prayer, for example victims of mass violence.

One may of course perform the ritual at their altar or designated sacred space, and it is also suitable to perform this rite outside after sunset. Should the outdoors be chosen, the libation will go into a hole you must dig just large enough to receive the libation. A cup or chalice will do fine if you wish to perform this at your altar. Bring an image of a pair of scales, or the Justice card of your preferred tarot deck. This is your focus, the symbol of the goddess who will be drawn up.

Light one to three bay laurel leaves (*Laurus nobilis*) and submerge them into a vessel of water before a lit candle that will represent the presence of Hestia. Wash your hands with the water. You have now made khernips. You may set this water aside just beyond the sacred space with another cup offering of wine or juice and give both to any profane spirits that hover near as appeasement that they may leave your ritual in peace.

The Gorgon's Guide

Present the offering libation of red wine, and if a substitution is required, pomegranate or grape juice will be fine. Pour this offering into the hole of the outdoor sacred space or the chalice of your altar. You may begin the recitation:

Sovereign Lady of the Underworld
Accept this, thine offering of the blood of thy son,
The Roaring One, Bull-Horned and Ivy-Crowned,
To hear my prayers on behalf of those harmed by
The hubris and defiance of those with power
But no humanity.

Praxidike! Who exacts Justice where people will not
Mother of the Kindly Ones, I pray open the gates
That your daughters may sweep the Earth from Tartarus
To seek those with rage and ill intent against the vulnerable,
To seek those with the false promise of protection,
To seek those with complicity in their hearts toward this hubris.

Let your daughters open every door in every realm for their prey
While you embrace the souls afflicted by the hand of Injustice,
Whether they dwell amongst mortals or reside in your country.
Embrace those who have suffered the loss that is brought by death.
Embrace those who have suffered the loss of autonomy and choice.
Embrace those who have suffered the loss of resources and community.

Keep us all in your embrace great lady, through our mortal journey to the end,
Where we pass the veil and rise within the realms to which we are sorted.
May we roar and rise as your son, unconquerable and blessed.

to Magical Resistance

If you wish to recite the names of individuals who have been harmed, do it now. If you have performed this outside, bring the khernips and wine or juice back to the sacred space and pour them into the hole before you fill it back in. Blow out Hestia's candle and gather your materials before you thank the gods and spirits. Then leave without looking back. For your own altar space, dispose of the libations as you would in accordance with your ritual customs.

Invoking the Ancestors of Revolution
A SPELL TO SUPPORT YOUR RADICAL DREAMS & ACTIONS
Lex Ritchie

ANCESTORS ARE OUR LINEAGE. The word lineage comes from Latin *linea* which has the literal meaning of string, line, thread. We usually reserve this word to refer to our ancestors of our blood lineage—a single line stretching through time. But lineage can also be a thread. And thread can be so much more than a line. Thread can be woven. This is a lineage of interconnection. And the fabric of that interconnection doesn't have to be blood. Lineage as thread can weave, knit, connect, and interconnect. Lineage is a woven web. It is the full tapestry of our lives and the lives of those who've cared for us. It is a knit garment created to keep us warm. It is the linen of the fine paper upon which dreams are inscribed.

Ancestor work is about honoring anyone you desire to honor who has contributed to who you are today. This can include your ancestors by blood, sure—your parents, and grandparents, and so on. But it also includes those you've learned from, those who inspire you, those who inform your worldview and your values, those whose words and wisdom guide your actions.

And connecting to those ancestors is about more than simply venerating them because they fucked and begat us and gave us life. Connecting to our ancestors of this woven web, and particularly our ancestors who explicitly shared our values and who worked for social change and justice in their lives, opens us up to a reservoir of strength, support, and vision that can sustain us in our own work for justice.

Working with our radical ancestors reminds us of the deep time of our struggle for justice, that we are just one small part in a grand collective effort. Your radical ancestors are waiting to support you, guide you, hold you as you take up and carry on their struggle.

to Magical Resistance

Here is a short spell for connecting to radical ancestors when you need the courage, inspiration, strength, or any other kind of support to keep working toward the better world you're dreaming of.

For this spell you'll need a book that is related to the collective of radical ancestors that you're seeking support from. Below I list a few suggestions of books that I have worked with, but any book that connects you to your anarchist, communist, queer liberationist, decolonial, radical trade unionist, etc. ancestors. The book is used for both bibliomancy and as a spoken offering for these ancestors. This spell uses a book because books are the bones of our ancestors' dreams. And it is these dreams for freedom and justice that we are picking up, adding our own dreams to, and carrying forward, step by step, making our collective dreams a reality.

Feel free to use or modify as you need. I suggest doing this spell in a western widow at sunset, but these are more like physical prompts that prime you for connecting to your ancestors. If you find it easy to connect to the dead, you feel called to do this spell elsewhere, or you're not able to do this spell in such a time or place, feel free to modify.

WHAT YOU NEED:

A western window

A sunset

A book from the radical tradition or one that fills you with hope. Books I have worked with: *Faggots and Their Friends between Revolutions* (Larry Mitchell, 1977), *Witchcraft and the Gay Counterculture* (Arthur Evans, 1978), *Another Mother Tongue* (Judy Grahn, 1984), *The Dispossessed* (Ursula K. Le Guin, 1974), and *Mutual Aid* (Dean Spade, 2020)

A candle

Your grimoire or journal

The Gorgon's Guide

Anything else you feel called to include (dirt, a meaningful stone, incense, a cup of water, etc.)

HOW TO DO IT:

As the Sun sets, place a lit candle in a west-facing window.

Connect to spirit how you choose and how feels right. Call on your guides, call on your radical or queer ancestors.

Light your candle and ask for the wisdom you're needing in this moment.

Take your book and, closing your eyes, open it to a random place. Run your finger along the page until you feel pulled to stop. Take the phrase, sentence, or paragraph you've landed on as wisdom to feed your radical action. Perhaps offer a reading from your favorite parts of this book up to your ancestors. Read aloud, and let your words move you, too. As your candle burns down sit with it, your card, your ancestors, and journal: pour out what you feel, integrate the wisdom you need. Then carry on, my revolutionary mystic, carry on your, our ancestors', our revolution. It is more vital, more potent, more powerful than ever.

Servitradis: A Servitor for Warning of Physical Danger
The Order of the Gorgon Shield

C REATED BY MEMBERS OF GORGON SHIELD, a group of magickal tech creators working towards the good of the polis. If you use this tech, please provide any feedback and/or experiences to aegis@gorgonshield.us.

ACTIVATION

To call upon Servitradis, look upon the sigil and speak the invocation. If the sigil is not physically handy, call up the image of it in your mind as clearly as you can. Then say:

Awaken Servitradis and warn me of personal danger in The Coming, the Soon, and the Now.

Repeat the words until you feel a connection to the servitor. Envision the eye opening, enlivening with energy that travels to the three concentric rings, then outward to the antenna. The energy empowers the sigil and connects to the servitor. Dismiss when you are out of the danger area.

Feel free to print the sigil and create a charm if you like. Do not modify the sigil.

To dismiss Servitradis, offer it your sincere thanks. Put some real emotion and energy into your gratitude. It is the energy that you give at the closing that helps to maintain the servitor.

WHAT SERVITRADIS DOES

Servitradis is a servitor that will warn you of potential threats within three zones identified as the Coming, the Soon, and the Now. The outer ring (the Coming) identifies threat warnings that can be evaded or provide time for preparation to engage it. The middle ring (the Soon) identifies threats that may or may not be avoidable but provide enough time to prepare for engagement. The innermost ring (the Now) identifies unavoidable threats that require immediate action. Use in any situation or location where you have a reasonable expectation of harm or danger. Please notice that the threat rings are not tied to distance, but to level of risk and opportunity for response.

TRAINING THE WARNING NOTIFICATION

Each person is unique in how they are attuned to their instincts, psychism, and situational awareness. When you first begin to use Servitradis it is important to instruct it and yourself on how you will be notified of the warnings it generates.

For example, envision a clear white field, like an artist canvas. Threats come as color from the direction of their source. Different threats have different colors and intensities and provide tracking if they cross through the various rings. Other options are to have it draw your gaze to where you need to look or hear a directional alert sound in your mind. Avoid using a general feeling or a sense of risk, as those are non-specific and might increase your anxiety which is counterproductive. This may take several calibrations until it works as you wish it to work.

to Magical Resistance

Bringing Sun to Earth
A TETRAD++IC PROTECTIVE AMULET

P. Sufenas Virius Lupus

THE CHRISTIAN FUNDAMENTALIST/DOMINIONIST THEOCRATS—
who have done so much to erode the rights of women in terms of women's own bodily autonomy—have set their sights next on abolishing the legal recognition of same-sex marriage. Even despite Congressional bills to help protect this right, state legislatures across the country have sought to criminalize treatment and recognition for trans (and, by extension, all gender-diverse) individuals, exclude them from sports and other activities, and much else besides. The theocrats claim that the presence and visibility of the modern LGBTQQPIA2SNB+ communities and individuals are "a sign of the End Times."

A broken clock can be right twice a day, and in this observation, I would assert they're absolutely correct—*but not in the way they believe.* The presence and visibility of queer people of all stripes in the modern world is not a sign of "the end of all things," but instead only of the "end" of the "times" when Christian hegemony has hemmed all public morality into narrow margins of enforced heteronormativity and strict gender dualist essentialism. In our advancing Age of Aquarius, their time has already ended, and though it may not feel like it at present, our mere visibility means we have already triumphed, and will be at the vanguard of the new aeon to come.

However, it is the dying donkey that kicks the hardest, and Christian hegemonic monotheism and all its attendant "moral" strictures still represent a kind of kick that will result in casualties of many kinds. If we can avoid those kicks, all the better; and if we cannot, then at least having some sort of armor to defend against their worst results will be beneficial.

The Gorgon's Guide

The Tetrad++ are a group of gender-diverse and eschatological Deities[1] Who first become known in early 2011, and Who continue in devotional relations to many individuals across the world, though those numbers may seem relatively small. The six core members of this group are aligned with particular gender-diverse identities: Panpsyche is a transwoman Goddess; Panhyle is a transman God; Paneros is a metagender/nonbinary Deity; Pancrates is a pangendered Deity; Paneris is a genderfluid Deity; and Panprosdexia is an agendered Deity. The six Tetrad++ Deities are also aligned to the Ephesia Grammata,[2] and Their influences can be invoked in conjunction with these most ancient and powerful names of Divine Grammatical Beings, which are some of the most widely attested of Ancient Greek and Græco-Egyptian *voces magicæ* formulæ.

Whether true or not, it is said that the Ephesia Grammata were carried as protective amulets in the ancient world written in gold letters,[3] and a Greek champion wrestler was even said to have been victorious because he carried them inscribed on a knucklebone.[4] Their following arrangement, in a non-canonical order, can coalesce and render accessible of the most protective and negativity-dispelling energies of the Sun to the material and practical substance of the Earth. Write them on a piece of papyrus, parchment, or at very least good card stock, preferably in gold-colored ink, but any ink that one may prefer will work.

The following spell includes an historiola, using the meanings of the Ephesia Grammata given by Androkydes (via Clement of Alexandria),[5] and should be recited aloud before and after writing the names. The Ephesia Grammata's names are transliterated into English and should be pronounced with long continental European vowels.

> ASKION KATASKION LIX TETRAX DAMNAMENEUS AISIA ENDASION
> ASKION KATASKION LIX TETRAX DAMNAMENEUS AISIA ENDASION
> ASKION KATASKION LIX TETRAX DAMNAMENEUS AISIA ENDASION
> *Paneros sent Eir All-Love across the cosmos in the light of the Sun,*
> DAMNAMENEUS.

to Magical Resistance

Panprosdexia's Shadow, KATASKION, *was Their filtration of love
through All-Acceptance.*
*Through the most treacherous tangles of the tails of comets—stars
which are Hairy,* ENDASION—*the light of love sent them streaming in a direction, averting their worst bindings and knotted
snares.*
Into and through the void of utter Shadowlessness, ASKION, *of the
unshaded soul of Panpsyche, that very love and acceptance spread
over Her All-Soul and into that of the greater cosmos.*
In the fullness of time in the Four Seasons, TETRAX, *Pancrates'
All-Power became manifest in Hir actions of protection and
preservation,*
and the True Voice, AISIA, *spoken by the tongue of Paneris, She/He of
All-Strife, to enlighten what is difficult and to illuminate all those
in turmoil.*
*Upon the fine brow of the bull-horned youth, Panhyle, His All-Body
and that of every material matter became suffused upon the
Earth,* LIX, *with the blessings of love, the protection of acceptance,
the presence of soul, the dynamism of power, and aversion of
strife—light into soil, warmth into stone, the Sun's indomitable
rays encompassing and enfolding the Earth and all beings upon
and within and above and of it.*
ASKION KATASKION LIX TETRAX DAMNAMENEUS AISIA ENDASION
ASKION KATASKION LIX TETRAX DAMNAMENEUS AISIA ENDASION
ASKION KATASKION LIX TETRAX DAMNAMENEUS AISIA ENDASION

Carry it, glance at it several times daily, and recite it in the order given whenever a difficult situation arises. Strengthen and guide yourself with the presence of these powerful Divine Beings—Who will be present, whether invoked or not invoked, through the words you carry.

We cannot be silenced and deprived of our True Voices (AISIA), shoved into the Darkness (ASKION) of closets, or kept in the Shadows

(KATASKION) from full visibility any longer; therefore, let us, in the flowering of the Four Seasons (TETRAX) in their turn, wear our Hair (ENDASION) as long or short or absent in as many colors as we may wish, as we bring the all-enlivening Sun (DAMNAMENEUS) down to the precious treasures—bodily and otherwise material—of this jewel called the Earth (LIX)!

As a wise spiritual musician once observed about the coming of the Sun, let us also take observance of the final results when the dying donkey stops kicking: "It's all right!"

NOTES

1. See P. Sufenas Virius Lupus, *All-Soul, All-Body, All-Love, All-Power: A TransMythology* (Anacortes: The Red Lotus Library, 2012), and further publications on Their evolving mythology and devotions to follow.
2. P. Sufenas Virius Lupus, *Ephesia Grammata: Ancient History and Modern Practice* (Anacortes: The Red Lotus Library, 2014); "At Sixes and Sevens: Further Thoughts on the Ephesia Grammata," in *Walking the Worlds* 3.2 (2017): 43–51.
3. Lupus, *Ephesia Grammata*, 51–52.
4. Ibid.
5. Lupus, *Ephesia Grammata*, 8–9.

to Magical Resistance

Consecrating a Protective Charm to the Gorgons and Hekate
River Enodian

IN ANCIENT TIMES, A SPECIAL AMULET, called a Gorgoneion, served as an apotropaic charm. Deities such as Athena and Zeus have been depicted wearing gorgoneions as a symbol of their power and ability to protect. Not unlike evil eye charms, gorgoneions were often worn to protect the wearer. They were also carved into buildings and put in important places to guard them, especially next to thresholds so that no evil could pass through.

Modern pagans and polytheists can find this symbol useful to protect them from harm. I have consecrated such a talisman in the name of the Gorgons and Hekate, goddess of witchcraft, liminal spaces, and the crossroads. Hekate is a goddess of the marginalized and the vulnerable, protector of children, and those who dwell in liminal spaces. Liminality refers to transitions and the space between places is a natural space for trans and/or non-binary folk to occupy.

You will need to find Gorgon depictions in the form of a coin, charm, or piece of jewelry. It doesn't have to be big, elaborate, or expensive. Also, it does not matter what it is made out of so long as it won't get damaged easily. You can consecrate more than one at a time, especially if you decide to wear one as a piece of jewelry, keep another by the door, hang another as a charm on your car mirror, etc.

Next create a working space to do the consecration. I did this from my altar to Hekate where I also have a shrine to the Gorgons. I was introduced to them through Hekate, and I feel that they make natural companions, especially for magical protective work. If you do protection magic regularly (which I recommend), you may want to consider an appropriate permanent or semi-permanent working space

You will need to provide offerings to both the Gorgons and to Hekate for the consecration. Burning incense should be sufficient, as frankincense was a common offering to Greek deities in ancient times. You can also do a libation of honey, wine, or olive oil. For Hekate you may also burn lavender, storax, or myrrh. For the Gorgons, either frankincense, storax, or myrrh are good. I prefer to burn loose incense on incense charcoal, so I can easily offer individual batches of incense to separate entities. If you decide to libate, have a bowl on hand to libate into, and pour it out onto the ground outside after the rite.

Either the dark Moon or the new Moon is an ideal time to do this. However, you can do this rite whenever you're able.

Have the talisman(s) ready that you wish to consecrate on the working space as well as the materials needed to make the offerings. You don't have to wear anything specific. Just wear what you normally do during any spiritual or magical working, and make sure that you wash your hands beforehand. It's traditional to make offerings to the Greek gods with washed hands.

To start, begin by reciting a prayer to Hekate. I'll use the Orphic Hymn to Hekate as translated by Apostolos N. Athanassakis as an example, but you can use any of the hymns or prayers found to Hekate online or in books:

> *Hekate Einodia, Trioditis, lovely dame, of earthly, watery, and celestial frame,*
> *Sepulchral, in a saffron veil arrayed, pleased with dark ghosts that wander through the shade;*
> *Perseis, solitary goddess, hail! The world's key-bearer, never doomed to fail;*
> *in stags rejoicing, huntress, nightly seen, and drawn by bulls, unconquerable queen;*
> *Leader, Nymphe, nurse, on mountains wandering,*
> *Hear the suppliants who with holy rites thy power revere, and to the herdsman with a favouring mind draw near.*

to Magical Resistance

After reciting, provide the offering to Hekate.
Next, call on the Gorgons. Here's my prayer to them:

Hail to the Gorgons: Stheno (sthey-no), Euryale (yoor EYE uh lee), Medusa!
Mighty, Far-Roaming, Queen!
Powerful goddesses whose gaze strikes fear and terror in their enemies!
Guardians against harm whose gaze stills all actions of evil!
Hear me, fierce Gorgons, and accept my offering in praise of you.

After reciting, provide the offering to the Gorgons.

Pick up the talisman to be consecrated. If you have more than one, repeat these steps and words for each item. You can also modify the wording to consecrate a talisman for someone else.

Holding the talisman in your hands, face east.

Mighty Hekate and fearsome Gorgons, bless and consecrate this
talisman that I may be protected from harm. In the East, I am protected.

Repeat this but with the appropriation direction being named, moving clockwise: face south, west, then north. When you're done turn to face your working space and hold the talisman above your head:

Mighty Hekate and fearsome Gorgons, bless and consecrate this
talisman that I may be protected from harm. Above, I am protected.

Hold the talisman low to the ground:

Mighty Hekate and fearsome Gorgons, bless and consecrate this
talisman that I may be protected from harm. Below, I am protected.

Hold the talisman over your heart:

Mighty Hekate and fearsome Gorgons, bless and consecrate this talisman that I may be protected in all directions from harm.
Fierce, powerful goddesses, bless and consecrate this talisman that my health, wealth, and home be protected.
Hekate, Gorgons, bless and consecrate this talisman that it may keep me out of harm's way in all areas of life.

To close the rite:

Mighty Gorgons, thank you for all that you have done and all that you continue to do. Accept this offering with my thanks and gratitude.

Provide the offering.

Mighty Hekate, thank you for all that you have done and all that you continue to do. Accept this offering with my thanks and gratitude.

Provide the offering.

CREATING A PROTECTION ALTAR

Protection work should be done as regularly as bathing, if not more frequently, and ideally you shouldn't wait for an emergency to do it. It's like insurance, there when you need it—and you never know when you will. This means that you need a space for such work, and that work is best done on a dedicated altar. Part of my altar to Hekate consists of a shrine to the Gorgons, and I pray to them often for protection.

If you are involved in activities which could put you in harm's way, are part of a marginalized group or groups, and/or partake of magic done to avert harm to other marginalized and vulnerable people regardless of whether it consists of baneful magic, you especially need to be doing protective work and often.

to Magical Resistance

For work you do regularly, you don't want it to be complicated or lengthy. One approach is to work in layers you can easily build upon. For example, perform one larger rite to initiate the work, and then do regular smaller rites. This is a good way to engage protective magic. It's not necessary to have a huge or elaborate space, just something that works.

For instance: my own altar to Hekate has:

- Statue of Hekate (pictures are also fine)
- Consecrated seven-day black candle
- Loose incense burner
- Decorative skeleton keys

And on one side of her altar:

- Statue of one of the gorgons
- Consecrated candle
- A small gorgoneion plaque

As you can imagine, this is compact, decorative, and utilitarian in honor of the goddesses. My supplies mostly come from the internet, or Azuregreen. Azuregreen is a fantastic resource for all pagans, occultists, and witches.

To begin, follow the initial steps of the Gorgoneion rite above: gather offerings, wash hands, and recite prayers to both Hekate and the Gorgons.

Next, address and talk to Hekate and the Gorgons—for as long as you need to. Let them know what you need protection for and why and ask them to help you. Be honest, open, and real—especially if you haven't done any formal work or worship with any of them before. Be sure to mention whatever practical work you are doing and have done, as Hekate helps those who help themselves. You can choose to write something in advance or write down the main points you want to address so you don't forget them.

To close the rite, follow the same closing as above, then;
Provide the offerings.

After the main rite, you can perform rites to them regularly in which you continue to thank them and ask for their help. You can do this daily, weekly, or often as you are able. If you are uncertain of how to do so and wish to keep it relatively formal, just do a standard format for an ancient Greek prayer. You greet the deity by name and titles, mention things you've done in the past for them and that they've done for you, make the request, then thank them. You can also reuse and/or modify the hymns and prayers provided earlier.

The Quartz Pentacle
A SPIRITUAL TOOL TO SUSTAIN THE WORK OF RESTORING THE WORLD

Enrique Gomez

THE WORK OF ANYONE INVOLVED IN ADVOCACY for justice and equality is draining. We at the Sylvan Hearth Pagan Temple wish to share a spiritual practice that we have developed to nurture and sustain those who work in transforming this world: The Quartz Pentacle. This tool can be used as a conceptual guide, a meditation tool, an antiphonal chant to unify intentions during a working, or a spiritual practice for shaping our individual actions. It could guide groups in the joint articulation of their goals, mission, and internal practices as well as strategic directions of community endeavors. The diagram of the Quartz Pentacle is represented below.

The Quartz Pentacle harmonizes five virtuous practices to create an inclusive community. At each point in the pentacle are the virtues of RESTORATIVE JUSTICE, RADICAL HOSPITALITY, DEEP LISTENING, IMPECCABLE BRAVERY, and COMPASSIONATE FORBEARANCE. These virtuous practices exist in a dynamic that requires an intentional and mindful practice from a community. The process of invoking this pentacle into a working involves tracing each virtue around the circle clockwise (*deosil*), while integrating the cross-positions of the other virtues to nurture an integral wholeness. Each virtue sustains another and is necessary for comprehensive healing.

RESTORATIVE JUSTICE

The virtue of Restorative Justice actively nourishes a community that has experienced trauma from oppression, harm, and discrimination. This practice orients the community toward health and wholeness. Restorative Justice names the harm done and gives victims the time and space to process that harm, to express themselves, and to find validation of their experience. It also offers those who cause harm a path to return to community if that is their choice.

RADICAL HOSPITALITY

The virtue of Radical Hospitality urges us to welcome both the stranger and the strange. Being mindful of our guests' backgrounds, spiritual practices, identities, and stage in life also allows us to anticipate and meet their needs. Creating welcoming spaces imbued with Radical Hospitality lets people know that their authentic selves can be celebrated and valued.

DEEP LISTENING

We practice the virtue of Deep Listening, which allows us to be receptive to voices with different and intersectional identities so that we may receive knowledge of their experiences. Deep Listening is essential to appreciative inquiry, which is the pathway to transformative dialogue.

IMPECCABLE BRAVERY

We practice the virtue of Impeccable Bravery so that when others point out misstatements in our speech or missteps in our work, we recognize how and why we erred and can come back to the community to

to Magical Resistance

practice what we have learned with new recognition and understanding. Impeccable Bravery is what we invoke when we create brave spaces and cultivate trust in our community.

COMPASSIONATE FORBEARANCE

In Compassionate Forbearance we draw from an inner stillness to pause so that the needs of the most silent of us become clear. We recognize that each of us speaks from a particular place of power, or the lack thereof, which also depends on the time and context of the moment. We lift the voices of marginalized people when we recognize our places of privilege and freely choose to actively step back, which allows them to be centered.

The Quartz Pentacle as a Dynamic Web

The Quartz Pentacle as a tool for meditation can help us elucidate how a network of virtuous practices can deepen our imagination of justice when facing the complexity of the world and its suffering. Here are five virtue patterns constructed by asking what each virtue needs as you trace the diagram around deosil, one virtue leading to another, and what virtues support another across the pentacle. The figure below offers an illustration of such a web of interrelationships.

The relationship arrows follow the pattern of an invoking pentacle found in various magical traditions and yield the following pearls of wisdom-practice.

> 1. "*As a builder of Restorative Justice, I need Compassionate Forbearance, and thus I discover within myself Impeccable Bravery.*" The ground that makes this Compassionate Forbearance possible is Impeccable Bravery. Impeccable Bravery is the necessary virtue when confronting the raw power of the state while opening spaces where we compassionately forbear the mechanical deployment of institutional power.

2. "*As a nurturer of Radical Hospitality, I require Restorative Justice, so I follow Compassionate Forbearance.*" Conversations about oppression and privilege get interrupted by the rhetoric of moral equivalence between groups of diverging privilege. Within the framework of Radical Hospitality, choosing to withhold moral equivalence arguments that only disrupt the Restorative Justice project rather than advance it is a form of Compassionate Forbearance.

3. "*As a healer of Deep Listening, I depend on Radical Hospitality, so I support Restorative Justice.*" When we choose to live in authentic community, we develop our capacity to hold each other's stories. Deep Listening helps us become discerning and expand our imagination of Restorative Justice. Radical Hospitality is what emerges when we are dedicated to Restorative Justice.

4. "*As a warrior of Impeccable Bravery, I seek out Deep Listening, so I practice Radical Hospitality.*" Impeccable Bravery is what allows us to ask what the needs of others are, and what in our behavior is keeping them from meeting those needs. Deep Listening is a path for discovering creative solutions that nurture ourselves as well as others that emerges from Radical Hospitality practice.

5. "*As a leader of Compassionate Forbearance, I am grounded by Impeccable Bravery, so I engage in Deep Listening.*" To compassionately forbear from excluding people is also one way we manifest our Impeccable Bravery in our world. Deep Listening shapes our moral understanding so that our Impeccable Bravery becomes rooted in a soil that is deeper and older than our ego project.

A worthwhile practice is to visualize the Quartz Pentacle in one's mind for a moment at the beginning of a new undertaking turning it into devotional work on behalf of freedom which transforms the structure of reality and makes us, as a community, invincible.

to Magical Resistance

Political Money Magic
Star Bustamonte

SOME OF THE MOST EFFECTIVE BANEFUL WORKINGS are those that incorporate an element that the subject of the working desires and will happily accept and not question. When it comes to political campaigns and politicians, the one thing they will joyfully accept is money. Financial support is what drives all campaigns because without it, they are dead in the water. Getting their message out, whether it is holding rallies, creating and airing commercials, mailings, or however they plan to connect with voters requires money. The amount of money required to run for even the lowest public office has become increasingly expensive.

One of the biggest mistakes frequently made when doing politically-oriented magical workings is to attack the organization or office. Most publicly held positions have protections built in that protect them to some degree from magical or spiritual influences. Hexing or cursing an organization is often akin to one person attempting to stand against a small army.

Focusing magical efforts on a single candidate is much easier than attempting to take on an entire political party. Whether the candidate is a newcomer to the political arena or an incumbent seeking to remain in office, they are all seeking funding for their campaign.

While much of the campaign funding collected is largely done online, and attaching a spiritual emphasis—for good or ill—to a digital transaction can be harder, it can be done. However, candidates running for office still hold multiple public events and they generally will take donations from pretty much anyone, especially when it is seen as being a grass roots, small donation.

Coins are the easiest to imbibe with magical energy since they are made from metal which often collects and holds onto the energy

The Gorgon's Guide

of the bearer or even those who have carried and handled it. Paper currency or any legal tender, like a check, can be written on using ink that is not visible.

My personal favorite is nightshade ink and using a selenite stylus to write the symbols or the essence of the spell on the bill for baneful workings. Lemon juice is also functional as an invisible ink that is only visible when exposed to heat. Any clear liquid, even charged water, can be used as "ink."

Consider the properties desired for whatever purpose is being sought and plan accordingly. Water charged by letting it absorb the energy of a stone or herbs is simple and something anyone can do. The water can also be placed under a full or dark Moon, and incorporating ritual aspects of personal practice can help further the energetic properties. It is as simple or as complicated as the practitioner wants to make it.

Simply stated, blessed or hexed money can be used to either help a candidate or harm their chances of getting elected when it is donated. Whether you are creating ink to use on some form of paper, legal tender, or placing the coins you intend to charge in the water or fluid, currency makes a great vehicle for magical energies since accepting currency signifies a contract.

It also can act as a contagion vector since the coin, bill, or check donated will be placed in with other currency which will pick up the vibration of the donated money. And as we all know, currency circulates, and as it does so, it continues to spread whatever energy has been attached.

☙ CHECKLIST FOR USING CURRENCY FOR POLITICAL PURPOSES:

1. Decide on the purpose—blessing or curse
2. Choose the type of currency to use
3. Create your "ink" or charge the coinage

to Magical Resistance

Next decide how to get the charmed donation into the hands and coffers of the campaign. There are several options and some of them will depend on how duplicitous the practitioner is capable of being.

Research ahead of time if there is rally or town hall scheduled and whether the campaign will accept cash donations on-site. In some cases, you could purchase a small piece of swag which could also be used for future additional magical workings.

If there is not a rally nearby, or it is not possible for whatever reason to attend one in person, there is likely a campaign office that will accept a donation. Of course, this means actually going into the office and interacting with whoever is there and staffing the office.

A number of groups that support any given candidate hold fundraising events to collect money and help disseminate the candidate's message. Attending one of these events and either giving directly or buying something small is another way to basically infect the money pool.

While mailing currency is generally discouraged, this is still an option for campaign contributions.

Whatever method is chosen, one thing that is certain is that no campaign will turn down even so much as a dime.

Magically charmed currency can be used to help a candidate or harm them, so it is fairly versatile.

The Reproductive Rights Sigil

Laura Tempest Zakroff

BUILT INTO THIS SIGIL:

❧ Protection of rights, services, people

❧ Increased accessibility to safe and legal procedures

❧ Health-minded focus

❧ Fact-based education about bodies, sex, pregnancy

❧ Body autonomy/respecting the sovereign self

❧ Removal of obstacles to safe/legal treatment for all

❧ Legalization secured permanently, not to be threatened or overturned.

WHAT TO DO WITH THIS SIGIL: This sigil is designed to aid in the protection of reproductive rights wherever they are under threat. Use in protests (signs and bodies), drawn it in appropriate places (health services, education centers), put it on candles, use on correspondence to health and legal institutions.

Tongues, Vulvas, and Open Eyes
APOTROPAIC MAGIC AGAINST PATRIARCHY

Rev. Christian Ortíz

APOTROPAIC MAGIC

The apotropaic concept (αποτρέπειν) is understood as any defense mechanism of a magical and transcendent order. It can be linked to an amulet, talisman, symbol, magic formula, drawings, and so on. One of its main characteristics is the power to expel undesirable and destructive influences. In a time where patriarchal hegemony threatens basic human rights, we deeply need the power to defend ourselves against the oppressive system and its emissaries. Historically, magic has been one of the resources most used by oppressed populations. It is a spiritual, symbolic, and cultural resource for the survival of identity and the recovery of power.

Simple and powerful symbols of apotropaic magic and traditional and modern practices are described here to be used in psychic and spiritual defense. In order for the apotropaic object to work, it must be activated. This step is mandatory, especially for talismans. A magical invocation can be made with the clear intention of awakening the magical memory that will endow it with power. It also functions as a deep meaning association and psychological exercise. Let us remember that magic is a complex process that manifests and lives in many dimensions. The object you choose to work with can be any jewelry (pin, ring, etc.). Prints, illustrations, drawings, ritual tattoos, or graphic representations are also common. The material is not so important, what is relevant is the presence of the magic symbol.

PREPARATION OF THE APOTROPAIC OBJECT

Select your object (drawing, jewel, ring, image, etc.). Invoke the sacred circle and the directions of the world. Cleanse the magical object with incense smoke, preferably on a new Moon, and recite the corresponding invocation.

MEDUSA: SHE IS THE POWER TO DEFEND OURSELVES

The figure of the gorgon Medusa is deeply linked to the traditions centered on the sacred feminine and the chthonic energies of the primordial goddesses. Working with her endows one with power and defensive strength, the ability to "paralyze" enemies, and provoke the return of anything evil.

INVOCATION:

Open eyes hunt you
heavy stone, become!
Without movement your body
it's fair you are tormented
Evil returned,
The job is done!

Now you can carry the amulet in your bag or wear it as a jewel. To protect a house or business, place it at the entrance of the house or attach it to the door. Allow your creativity, intuition, and needs to guide you. You can give it to a person who experiences harassment, violence, or attacks. It has great defensive power in cases of violence and abuse against women, girls, and people of sexual diversity.

BAUBO: SHE IS THE POWER TO ENJOY

Patriarchy uses guilt and shame to control people's bodies and minds. Its insidious and toxic effect is transgenerational. Baubo is a loving bridge that allows us to return to the right not only to survive, but to really live in sacred pleasure and joy. It is not enough to survive a predatory system, resistance is also to enjoy and prosper.

to Magical Resistance

Baubo is an "obscene" and playful deity who represents the power of sacred laughter, happy bodies, and sex. Her symbol is used to ward off guilt, evil criticism, and unhealthy judgments. She is represented as a woman showing her genitals, or even simply as a vulva.

INVOCATION:

I expel your cruel words,
inside and outside of me.
Perfume of life I invoke,
world of laughter I invoke.
In perfect order,
so the wheel turns!

You can work with this amulet daily to expel destructive influences that create guilt, sadness, shame, and other painful states. Place it in the bedroom or bathroom, near a mirror. Cast out horrible judgments that destroy self-love. Patriarchy also lives within us, and it is necessary to expel it from the core. You can give the amulet to people who are struggling to love and accept themselves, who are in the process of healing and dignity. It is a good resource for people who have been attacked for exercising their sexuality. Baubo connects us with the sacred right to live in diverse and joyful bodies.

KALI: SHE IS THE POWER OF TRANSFORMING RAGE

Goddess Kali's tongue is impressively powerful and frightening. It represents a threatening and fierce energy. There is a divine right to transformational rage, thanks to Her we can free ourselves from oppression and abuse. She is the bridge that connects us with our healthy defense instincts, which have been silenced by a system that wants submissive and docile people. She is a "stop" to any form of abuse.

INVOCATION:

Oh, Lady of Rage!
Justice I invoke
May the enemy never rest
may his body and soul shattered
Hands and legs be tied
pain in all his flesh
With no rest or consolation,
It's done! without hesitation.

This amulet is recommended for cases of attack and violence. The apotropaic power of this symbol is sharp and direct. It can be used to protect our house, but also to return the evil that has been done. It is appropriate in defensive magic and can be tied with a black ribbon to the photograph or article of clothing of an enemy who has wronged us.

Our altars and magical spaces are not only spaces of devotion, they are also healing and political spaces, in them we also work trauma, healing, pain and anger. It's time to take back our power, now more than ever.

As above, so below,
As within, so without.
May the power be ours
Be in love ... and in rage.

to Magical Resistance

The Rite of Abominations
A SACRAMENT OF SACRED TERMINATION

Georgia van Raalte

Oh Holy Whore, Our Lady of the Darkness, She Who is the Terminatrix. Give us Thy Fury, Thy Rage, Thy Voice. Grant us the force of a thousand volcanoes, the nimbleness of the rivers, the inevitability of the sea. To those who shoulder this burden, grant to them Thy Strength, and the darkest of Thy Glories.

ABORTION IS SACRED, A HOLY ACT in which we affirm our Godhood, in which we manifest our embodied divinity through choice—a choice with which we declare that we are not slaves or chattel, with which we declare we are not rocks or bones or spirits or souls but bodies, the solidification of divinity into its most perfect form—a form which is not eternal, but a constant flux and cycle which is the true nature of God. When we choose abortion, whether in a hospital, a back alley or in a bathroom stall, we become God. This, of course, is why the act is so feared by those who do not understand, by those who do not know what it means to be divine. It is a harrowing thing, a sad thing, a hard thing—and this is the confirmation of its sacred nature. A sacrifice is meaningless if it doesn't hurt. We sacrifice this potential for our now. This pain for our joy. In the act of abortion we become arbiters of our own future and our own physicality.

THE RITUAL

I invoke thee Holy Whore and Mother of Abominations.
Reside with me, of Timeless One who art seated upon the Throne of
   Eternity.
Stay my feet and guide my hands as I complete this holy, obscene rite.

The Gorgon's Guide

Bless this medicine, oh Dark One.
Bless this Pharmakon, that I might feel thy movement and thy shaking.
Hold me in Thy womb, as I undertake this rite to excavate mine.

I recognise the sanctity of my Body.
I recognise the sanctity of the Earth
I recognise that there is no difference.
We are continuous, Effluvium of the Earth.

I choose to be a mover.
I choose to make change.
I choose to enact authority over my own body, and there is no will nor law that can compel me otherwise.

I consume the Sacrament.
I honour this outward sign of my inner grace.

Holy Holy Holy! All things that creep and crawl and are consumed are holy.

The deed is done. The snake has eaten its tail. The tower falls. A new world rises from its wreckage.

The blood begins to pour, to spill. Every drop which flows is a drop which is sanctified, made holy in Her Cup of Abominations.

Fill Her Cup. Fill it unto the brim with this most holy substance.

Raise the cup to Her, an offering to the Holy Whore who sits upon the Throne of Eternity.
Raise your cup, and offer to Her your sacrifice.
Offer Her your pain and your shame, your red blood and your chains.

to Magical Resistance

See in Her ancient eyes a mirror. Know yourself divine.

Sing unto Her: My Lady!
Within this cup is the flesh of my flesh, the blood of my blood. This sacred admixture do I offer unto you, my Lady. As my sorrow is Your sorrow, so is Your joy my joy.

[Burn or bury the sacrament as you feel called to do. Finish with a prayer:]

Oh Mother Babalon,
My Goddess who art like a city or a mountain, holy art Thou, Oh Lady.
All dirt and all things rotting. All blood and things which pour. All those rejected, all those who fear, all those who seek respite.
May they find the sanctity of your embrace.

The Gorgon's Guide

to Magical Resistance

The Phallus Tree
AN HISTORICAL ARTIFACT AND A CONTEMPORARY INSPIRATION

Cory Thomas Hutcheson

AT THE FOOT OF A LATE MEDIEVAL ILLUMINATED MANUSCRIPT known as *Roman de la Rose* (*The Romance of the Rose*) a curious-looking, brown-robed nun reaches to pluck something from a tree and drop it into her basket. The "fruit" of this particular plant happens to be a collection of penises, all white with bright red tips. Four remain in the foliage, while at least two are already in her basket.

The *Roman de la Rose* was a popular French poem on the qualities of love, but it was also regarded as sensual and a lascivious, and additional images such as nuns and monks engaged in passionate embraces or even a "nun leading a monk by a chain attached to his penis" all adorn the extra-textual reaches of the pages in some copies.[1] Additionally, stories of nuns and monks violating their celibacy oaths were also widely popular, and bawdy stories like these appear in Chaucer's work, *The Canterbury Tales* (Chaucer himself may even have done a translation of the *Roman*). So what's going on with these penis trees?

This bit of marginalia—the extracurricular doodling done by many manuscript illuminators with figures ranging from everyday people to rabbits jousting on the back of snails (because illuminating was time-consuming and often tedious so why not have a little fun?)—may seem strange, but the "phallus tree" was a common motif. Dozens of examples exist showing these trees bedecked with phallic shapes, sometimes with women or birds perched nearby to pluck them, and sometimes all by themselves. They are drawn in ink on vellum, painted in frescoes on walls, carved in wood, and even cast in metal as—of all things—pilgrimage badges!

The meaning of these penis-plants has never been one hundred percent explained, but that hasn't stopped eager conjecture about them.

The Gorgon's Guide

Sexual health scholar Johan Mattelaer puts forth the theory that these images concern fears about male impotency and witchcraft. He notes that popular belief in parts of Europe during the Middle Ages suggested that nuns were some of the most likely candidates for practicing witchcraft— a theme echoed by works like Giovanni Boccacio's 14th-century collection of tales, legends, and lore known as *The Decameron*. Mattelaer links the works of witchcraft outlined in other medieval texts like the infamous *Malleus Maleficarum* and points out that many men—especially those holding positions of clerical power—feared that women would turn to witchcraft as a way to control them and rob them of that power. Witches might turn into the birds depicted in phallus trees like those on the fresco of the Fonte Nuovo fountain in Tuscany to screech into bedrooms of men and spirit their manhoods away, ultimately hanging them in trees where they would wither and leave their owners impotent.[2]

While we can only speculate on the role of these phallus trees historically for the time being, this thread of witchery and sorcerous power-theft leaves open a question of, "well, why not?" After all, for those inclined to witchcraft and magic, why not look to these sorts of images for inspiration, especially in eras where power is unevenly wielded by institutions or gender conglomerates? If a witch sees men in power where they shouldn't be, exercising control over affairs that are frankly not their business to begin with, why not "erect" a phallus tree of one's own?

I am not advocating a guillotining of literal private parts here, but a tapping into the bird imagery in some of these depictions. After all, it would take little effort to rinse out a condom thoroughly (to remove any lubricants or potentially harmful chemicals), fill it with birdseed and lightly melted peanut butter or coconut oil, and let it set in the freezer with a string run down the center. Silicone molds of penises used for bachelorette cakes and other festivities could also work just as easily, and if you have access to those you can even bake your molds to

to Magical Resistance

make them hold together better using a binder like stiffened egg whites. One could even write the name of a person or two or six, shred them to bits, and add them into the mix![3] Then they might hang those lovely seed phalluses in their nearest tree to be pecked apart by hungry birds, feeding them and nourishing them (and the squirrels who will inevitably find a way to get to them, too, with their sharp rodent teeth). A good work done to feed the wild things of the world, and a spell to dismantle the "rod" of power being used to oppress.

Soon one could have phallus tree of one's own, and without all those pesky vows of chastity and obedience that comes with joining the local nunnery. A perfect addition to any witch's garden.

NOTES

1. "Nun Harvesting Phalluses from a Phallus Tree and a Monk and Nun Embracing," on *Feminae: Medieval Women and Gender Index*, University of Iowa, 2014 (https://inpress.lib.uiowa.edu/feminae/DetailsPage.aspx?Feminae_ID=31987)
2. Johan Mattelaer, "The Phallus Tree: A Medieval and Renaissance Phenomenon," *The Journal of Sexual Medicine* 7.2 (2010): 846–51.
3. While most birdseed should be fine in this application, if one is inclined to try this, it can be good to avoid birdseed mixes with invasive species' seeds in the mix, so as to avoid crowding out native plants.

The Gorgon's Guide

Everyday Hexes and the Publicly Contested Body, or,
HOW TO GET CLEAN TO DO THE DIRTY WORK

Jessica Della Janare

A MEMORY: IT IS AUGUST and my partner and I are sitting on the beach. Bonfires are being lit, the water is filled with boats, and the sun is just starting to set. It is, in a word, idyllic. Suddenly, a volleyball comes out of nowhere and slams the back of my head. I scream—equally in surprise and in trauma response—and the person whose serve went awry jogs the twenty yards from the volleyball net to retrieve his ball. I expect something of an apology. Instead? He looks at me and says "fat fucking bitch, you shouldn't even be here."

I don't remember what I did next. I'm sure I cried. I'm sure I seethed. I hope I grounded. What I didn't do, though, is the one thing I should have done: run into the sea. Aside from the fact that freezing cold salt water would have stimulated my vagus nerve and soothed my nervous system, it would have quickly and effectively cleared that hex away.

Wait. Was that a hex?

Consider flower essences. These incredibly diluted preparations carry the energetic signature of the plant they were made from. Despite their dilution, they are an incredibly effective treatment for any number of energetic or psychic imbalances. What would a hex look like if its energetic signature were equally diluted? It would look like a microaggression. A projection. Mansplaining. Side eye.

- The person with the sign outside the abortion clinic is hexing you.
- The cops holding the lines at the protest are hexing you.
- The co-worker who perpetually mis-pronouns you is hexing you.
- The person calling you a fat bitch is hexing you.

to Magical Resistance

The list goes on. Are these everyday hexes precise? No. Are they diluted? Definitely. But they can quickly accumulate and take a toll on our hearts, psyches, and magic.

If it seems like everyday hexes are insidious, that's because they are. Moreover, publicly contested bodies are more susceptible to everyday hexes because we represent a type of freedom and liberation most people can only dream of.

I use the term "publicly contested body" to refer to those of us who have become accustomed to hearing our very right to existence debated on the news or in public forums. I also use this term to recognize that our relationships to the "public" is constantly in flux. A cis white gay man in rural Utah will have a very different experience than in San Francisco's Castro District; a Black trans woman, unfortunately, may not.

Magically, the phrase "publicly contested" provides an important alternative to "marginalized." The margins are where the witch lives and works. She has always tended the edges of culture, weaving and carving the world to be. Our currents and currencies are world shaping power; everyday hexes seek to rob us of them.

In times of crisis, our magic needs to be three things: flexible, adaptable, and effective. Which brings us to spiritual bathing. Spiritual bathing is a practice of mindful, intentional washing away psychic detritus using a combination of water, plants, minerals, and prayer. It is a simple but effective tool that allows you to lovingly tend to both your physical and psychic biomes.

I write this from a perspective of a very fat white queer femme witch settled in a large city in the so-called United States. Although numerous studies have shown that the belief that fat people smell more than thin people is nothing more than poorly disguised fatphobia, I'm accustomed to the cultural messaging that says the way my body is inappropriate. When I first learned the concepts of magical bathing, my Taurus Sun dug in her heels to resist. I thought I was saying that I have the right to smell however I smelled; what I really was saying was that I had a right to humanity that dominant culture has sought, again and again, to rob me of.

But my spiritual bathing practice taught me that it isn't about washing away my humanity. In fact, it's the exact opposite: by folding it into my pre-existing adornment rituals, it has become a vital opportunity to relish in embodiment and recalibrate my personal echo- and ecosystems back to neutral, allowing me to do more effective magic.

There are countless traditions of spiritual bathing, and, as such, countless herbs and allies you might reach for—and, truly, just as many as you should not. I encourage you to find practices that your ancestors can recognize. Learning those traditions is one of the many ways to build relationships with them, and those relationships are the foundation of so much that witches. Researching the spiritual bathing practices of the Italian peninsula taught me about bathing rituals *l'acqua di San Giovanni* and the Feast of the Madonna of the Baths: two ancestral traditions that have become the highlight of my magical year.

If you don't know where to begin, consider the obvious: salt water. Hexes are more likely to accumulate at the base of the skull and anywhere where skin touches skin, such as behind the knees, armpits, fat rolls, genitalia, and underneath breasts. If a bathtub is inaccessible to you, consider a bowl of water and a ladle.

Remember, too, that nature abhors a vacuum: when you clear things away, make sure to intentionally fill that psychic space with something that serves you. Rose for love and softening. Basil for prosperity and luck. Rosemary for protection. Your energetic ecosystem is yours to care for and tend, and doing so will make you less susceptible to hexes in the future.

You are not responsible for other people's stories about you. You are not required to carry them. You are, however, responsible for what you do with them. Spiritual bathing is just one of many practices that will free up your lifeforce for the great work of culture changing that we're all being called to do.

to Magical Resistance

Hail to the Women

Heka deAuset

I will not be quiet,

My spirit won't let me.

She will not let these horrors

Being perpetrated on women

As the way it will continue to be.

She will not be broken by tragedy,

She knows that it is

The fire that forges the blade.

She knows she can never be destroyed.

She screams her battlecry from with the flames

Let me be transformed,

I welcome change.

I will not stand silent,

My dead sisters will not let me.

Holding onto a single symbolic flame,

Voices of women gone too soon.

Their fires extinguished in brutal acts of violence

By men who once professed their love.

Out of the darkness of the infinite,

The Gorgon's Guide

They speak to me,
Not one more life brought back to me this way,
Not a single one.

I will not lower my voice
When lies are being told,
The truth will not let me.
The truth has always been,
You are beautiful, you are wise,
You are strength and love,
You are a powerful mystery.
You are peace and pleasure,
Untamed and free.
Infinite.

So hail to the women,
And blessed may you always be.

to Magical Resistance

The Truth Speaks Sigil
Laura Tempest Zakroff

BUILT INTO THIS SIGIL:

- Revelation of Truth
- Clarity/Clear Signal
- Movement of Information in the Correct Direction
- Healing/Health-Focused
- Foster Critical Thinking/Discernment
- Encourage Positive Action (things that help, not hurt)
- Community Mindful – being more conscious that we're all interconnected, to look out for everyone not just the self
- Increase Compassion & Empathy

WHAT TO DO WITH THIS SIGIL: This sigil fights misinformation, clearing the way for truth to speak and allow it to be heard. Carve or place on a candle to help foster truth, direct the energy to community, local government, media, use in protests to amplify the message, use in scrying and divination to uncover what's blocking truth, as well as a ward.

To Curse in the Name of Nemesis
EXCERPTED AND LIGHTLY ADAPTED FROM *Orphic Hymns Grimoire*

Sara Mastros

THE ORPHIC HYMN TO NEMESIS

I cry out to Nemesis: Goddess, All-Seeing Queen,
Who sees into the hearts of all mortal beings.
Eternal One, exceedingly venerable, holy, august
Delighting in Dike, mighty ally of the just.
Shape changing, quick shifting, eternally dynamic,
Chaotic, confusing, perhaps even erratic,
Your Word's ever changing and under discussion,
A long winding road, but arcing toward justice,
For you hear every care in the hearts of mankind,
And the fear of you weighs on each mortal mind.
The overproud psyche, and the promiscuous liar,
Can try to escape you, but find no safe harbor.
You see all, you hear all, you judge every lie,
Justice dwells in your heart, oh daemon most high.
Come, blessed one, ally of mystics, friend of the wise,
Give wings to good intentions, cut down hateful lies.
Replace unhallowed thoughts and contemptuous feeling
stop the fickle, flip-flopping wheeling and dealing.
Blessed goddess of fairness, heed our cry,
And to your task, mighty Nemesis, fleetly fly.
To Curse in the Name of Nemesis

WHO IS NEMESIS?

Nemesis (Νέμεσις) is the Greek goddess of reparations. She is a twin to Tyche, the goddess of fortune. Her name derives from the word for "fair distribution"; Nemesis is the righteous anger that unfairness

to Magical Resistance

engenders, and the just retribution that punishes it. Nemesis balances the scales when luck is too unfair. When she is properly understood as the goddess that punishes inequity, Nemesis is restored as a glorious and powerful goddess of the people. That her name, in our speech, has come to mean "enemy" is a byproduct of how deeply fucked up our culture is. We have been trained to believe that Nemesis is our enemy, but she is the goddess who upholds equity and punishes unfairness. Who, I wonder, might have means, motive, and opportunity to disempower her in that way?

BEGINNER SUGGESTIONS FOR CURSING:

› Choose your target carefully, name them precisely, and link to them as tightly as possible. Do not try to curse large groups of people, or abstract forces.

› There are forces lying in wait for your invitation to do harm, and those forces are just as happy to hurt you as someone else. Do not accidentally invoke spirits of blind rage, hate, or vengeance. They will fuck you up.

› The Moon, when waning, is good for bane-ing.

› Mercury retrograde is the slay curser's aid.

› Mars direct, the just protects.

A BEGINNER'S CURSE (*experienced magicians, modify as desired*)

⭆ SUPPLIES

❡ Your target's full name & video of them
❡ An ikon of Nemesis
❡ A black magic marker
❡ A white 7-day candle, not in a jar
❡ A bowl of salt water

The Gorgon's Guide

¶ Straight pins
¶ About an hour
¶ $13 in cash

WHAT TO DO

1) Compose a letter to Nemesis, explaining the injustice you are asking her to address.

2) Write the target's name on the candle.

3) Enter into magical time, space, and consciousness in your usual fashion.

4) Ritually baptize the candle as the target.

5) In your most magical voice, read aloud the hymn to Nemesis.

6) Search your heart for guilt in the matter at hand. Confess any wrong you have done, and then cleanse yourself in your usual manner.

7) Read your letter outloud to the candle.

8) Watch the video. Feel rage build. Keep the video playing for the rest of the spell.

9) Put the candle in a bowl of salt water, and light it.

10) Slowly read the hymn out loud again, while sticking pins in the candle.

11) Say "Nemesis, I charge you, by the time this flame goes out, right the scales of justice. In payment for this, I offer $13."

12) Sit with Nemesis and listen as well as you can to what she has to say.

13) Return to normal time/space/consciousness in your usual fashion.

14) Before the candle goes out, distribute the $13 to at least three different beggars. Look them in the eye, smile and bless them when you give them the money. If you absolutely cannot do this, you may give $39 to a charity which supports the unfortunate instead.

15) When you are done giving away the cash, wash your hands and fully disconnect from the curse.

to Magical Resistance

NEMESIS

ΝΕΜΕΣΙΣ

© Brian "Chase" Charles, illustrator of *Orphic Hymns Grimoire* (Hadean Press, 2022).

The Gorgon's Guide

Uerymurc: A Servitor for Undermining Harmful Communication
The Order of the Gorgon Shield

WHAT IS UERYMURC?

Servitors are magical artificial intelligences created with particular parameters and for specific purposes. Uerymurc (pronounced *YURI-murk*) was created by the Order of the Gorgon Shield with the intention of disrupting communication that threatens the peaceful. This includes subverting chains of command when there is action against the peaceful; undermining the efficacy of communication meant to inspire or organize violence or harm; and opposing aspects of our media ecosystem that encourage violent extremism.

Most extremists are radicalized, recruited, and organized through the internet, although that is not the sole pathway to radicalization. Uerymurc has been effective in actions that counter aspects of this ecosystem—including de-platforming, strengthening the resolve of major providers to refuse to carry certain platforms that are designed to spread hate, and so forth. Anything that undermines the efficacy of hateful extremists from being able to recruit and organize is important. Uerymurc has also been used to undermine the communications coming from specific hate organizations and in other media—such as television—and has been tested in undermining the messages of public officials that they had intended to use to weaken democracy.

INBUILT PROTECTIONS

Because of the level of judgment required by Uerymurc, safeguards were built into its creation. The most important is that Uerymurc was created under the aegis of Hermes/Mercury, and any order given to this servitor can be countermanded by this Great One. Another important protection is that Uerymurc will "go to sleep" three days after last being called and will dissipate three years after the last time they are called.

CONSIDERATIONS FOR WORKING WITH UERYMURC

When giving Uerymurc a charge, we recommend that you make it reasonably specific. If it is an in-person threat—specify that. A charge should include a clear vision of what success looks like. For example, rather than just telling Uerymurc to fix misinformation, it will be more efficacious to tell them to work on holding platform x accountable for the way their product is used to incite violence or to drive platform y to change the way their recommender engine works so radicalizing material isn't recommended. These charges are clear and accomplishable.

↣ ACTIVATION OF UERYMURC

1. Call to Uerymurc—the short version is the necessary call.

2. Raise energy and tell Uerymurc that it is for them.

3. Give Uerymurc a specific charge in alignment with their purpose.

4. Thank Uerymurc and send them off.

CALL TO UERYMURC (*short version*):

Uerymurc AWAKEN! Lord of Garbled Confusion, I set you upon those who threaten the peaceful.

EXAMPLES OF LONGER CALLS (*add specifics*):

An in-person threat:

Uerymurc AWAKEN! Lord of Garbled Confusion, I set you upon those who threaten the peaceful. Protect me here and now against those who threaten us. May none understand the other. May they fall into disarray—their energy dissipating in confusion. May their meaning be lost. May they work at cross-purposes to each other, blocked at every turn, tripping over each other. May none be hurt, but may my adversaries break-ranks and withdraw. And then, Uerymurc, we will honor you as a peacemaker.

For use on the toxicity on the Internet:

Uerymurc AWAKEN! Lord of Garbled Confusion, I set you upon those who threaten the peaceful. Flow through the network, through the cables, connections and servers and bollix up all that incites violence, that incites hatred, or that spreads lies. Make their creators bungle everything and their energy dissipate in impotent confusion. And then, Uerymurc, we will honor you as a peacemaker.

to Magical Resistance

A Thought-Form for Disruption
Philip Kane

TO BEGIN, and to contextualise the ritual working that follows, I should start by mentioning the sources from which the process has evolved.

Long, long ago (in 1987 or '88, to be a little more precise), there was a magazine called *Moonshine,* in the pages of which the late Rich Westwood published an article outlining what he called a "political ritual." That ritual was very quickly adopted and adapted by my coven, spawning a number of variations over the years as we've worked with it. Besides that influence, I've drawn upon a series of activities undertaken by the London Surrealist Group (of which I'm a member), some years ago to "summon the spirit of Spring Heeled Jack," who we had deemed to be the spirit of London chaos. I should write a full account of that project someday, probably with a health warning attached, but for now, suffice to say that lessons have been learned and absorbed, and the less hazardous aspects are included in this working.

So much for the necessary preamble. The working that follows here is intended to summon, or create, and then activate a thought-form with the specific purpose of disruption, or alternatively of *stirring the cauldron* within a community.

Quite how "community" is defined, in the latter case, is flexible. It might relate to a geographical location, although that can complicate matters as physical spaces are might be inhabited already by various Power Beings. Just taking my own urban home locality as an example, we have a minor river goddess and an assortment of Power Beings associated with springs, with woodland, and even with particular trees. Introducing a new entity without first gaining agreement from all of those would be rather like bringing an uninvited guest along to an invitation-only party; bad manners, at best.

The Gorgon's Guide

More effectively, the thought-form might be introduced into (as examples) the LGBTQ+ community in your town or city; a union branch/local; a group of environmental activists; a local community group working with the homeless. The list could go on, but that should hopefully suffice to give an idea of the range of possibilities. Naturally, it is not ethical to *impose* a created thought-form onto such communities without some degree of collaboration. Do involve at least some people who are actually a part of the community you wish to effect, especially if you are not already involved and a part of it yourself.

This working can be a good way to shake things up and disrupt the status quo within a community that has become stale, conservative, or apathetic.

It can also be used as a means to cause deliberate disruption—say, to a water company that's dumping sewage into a river, a building development that involves destruction of ancient woodland, or a fascist organisation. Again, these are merely limited examples to give some idea of the range of possibilities. In such circumstances, obviously the above remarks about collaboration do not stand.

For clarity, I've separated the process of the working into a series of distinct steps. In practice, you might find that the stages flow together less distinctly. Anyway, onto the working itself...

▷ **STEP 1:** Preliminaries. Decide on the focus for the working. Be clear about the fact this is a magical working, that it requires some effort, and that it will have consequences in the real world, at least some of which will likely be unexpected.

▷ **STEP 2:** Create a visual representation of the thought-form. There are traditional approaches that can be used—dream incubation, trance, and so on. Maybe there is even, in some cases, a pre-existing entity with visual images already representing it, that can be called upon (for instance, as was the case with Spring Heeled Jack). However, a technique that can work well as a means of creating a visual image for a

to Magical Resistance

new thought-form of this type is the Surrealist drawing game of *cadavre exquis* or "exquisite corpse." At root an adaptation of the old game of Consequences, this enables a collective channel through which an image can emerge from the participants' unconscious.*

☞ **STEP 3:** Define some other characteristics of the thought-form. This can be done via questions and answers, automatic writing, or even a form of roleplay. Name it (this is important); and together, create a sigil or other symbol that contains the *essence* of the thought-form.

☞ **STEP 4:** Define a geographical location where the thought-form will be centred. Ideally, this should be a place of some significance to the target. But if there isn't such a place, look for somewhere that seems to fit with the "character" of the thought-form—it might be a natural feature, but in an urban environment could just as easily be a patch of so-called wasteland, or even a bus shelter. If setting out to create disruption to the target, then the locus might be, for instance, a company office or a building site.

☞ **STEP 5:** Now we come to the ritual working itself. Bring the working group together in a convenient place. Cast a Circle by your preferred means. This can be done quite informally, especially if using a public space or if there are people in the group who are not familiar with the practice. Raise energy, again using your preferred method. Collectively, visualise the symbol of your thought-form in the centre of your Circle. "See" it growing. Together, lift it up and see it moving until it hovers above the place where you wish the thought-form to be centred. Then lower it, see the symbol merge with the place. Visualise the thought-form itself emerging in its location. Finally, close down the ritual and ground yourselves appropriately.

And finally . . . This is—for reasons of space as much as flexibility—a very abbreviated recipe. It leaves practitioners to do some research, and adjust the process according to taste and context.

*An excellent source for this and other Surrealist games is *A Book of Surrealist Games*, by Alastair Brotchie (Shambhala, 1993).

Loki mask, digital and Posca paint pen, K.A.H., 2022.

to Magical Resistance

Masks of Our Time
K.A.H

WE TEND TO VIEW the *mask* in simple ways. As entertainment, the term evokes nostalgic memories of Halloween costumes or creative associations with adult cosplay. As a negative metaphor the mask can signify forced hiding, repression, deception, or lies. Someone can use a mask to trick others, engage in criminal behavior, or enact cruelties. To *mask* indicates disguise or protection, which points to a world in which such concealment is necessary. Our contemporary experience has shown us the mask as a kind of armor against infection and its spread, but it has also become a focus of political conflict. There are those who have vigorously rejected masks as oppressive tools.

These associations with masks speak to a reality that is simple and fixed. What if masks reveal our experience to be mutable or even volatile? Masks and masking involve transformation, alteration, and manipulation of form (Danielsson, 2007). In western culture we can view the mask as a crafted object that appears in liminal spaces: a death mask preserves the life-like features of one who is newly deceased, a theatrical mask bridges the space between actor and audience, a veil can mark the transition from single to married or married to widow. This perception of masks induces a different kind of fear. The liminal, the space between, is an uncomfortable place. Although it is a site of possibility, it is also a site of confusion or chaos. In film, a bridging shot covers a break in continuity between sequences. It is neither the former sequence nor the latter, but it helps viewers understand the narrative's transition. As liminal objects, masks connect and reveal. Like metaphor, they help us to understand what is too complicated or beyond rational explanation. More than just revelation or spectacle, though, masks are spaces for transformation.

This potential for transformation speaks to my need for wonder and transcendence. My bookshelves contain an assortment of books on masks: African cultures, European village festivals, the Italian commedia, Ralph Meatyard's photography, and museum exhibit catalogs just to highlight a few. More recently I have started studying and drawing Norse masks from artifacts that are reproduced in art history texts, current archaeological articles and publications, and guides to Viking ornament. Consulting these sources and more, I enjoy creating my own variations on the common mask forms found on runestones and artifacts. In my paintings, I tend to give an identity to the masks; a crossed-out eye is Odin, and a stitched mouth makes obvious reference to Loki.

Mention Loki's name, and it will be met with venom that rivals the dripping fangs of the snake under which he is bound; however, Loki has emerged in contemporary consciousness in striking ways. The Marvel character (in its variety of storylines) is the obvious example; however, he has become a queer icon as well for numerous reasons. He is a shapeshifter; he is a mother to Sleipnir and a father to Hel, Fenrir, Jormungandr, Vali, and Narvi. Many people who feel disenfranchised, erased, or live on the margins of mainstream society find him to be an inspiring figure. Those who experience threats of violence or loss of basic human rights look to Loki's disruptive quality. Although the words *chaos* and *mischief* appear too often, the concept of destabilization applies well overall. His identity is fluid, not fixed. It is no wonder he is hated by those who find ambiguity threatening to their status quo. My drawing of Loki (see fig. on p. 68) shows the result of my basic process. I will draw the entire mask, or I will draw half and double the image in Photoshop, which is not a true split representation found in Viking craft, but similar.

EXERCISE

In many cultures, gods, entities, ancestors, and various elemental forces have been represented by masks and performance accoutrements. Design your own mask to provide form to whatever is valuable to you; the mask could also be the identity you wish to "grow into" in these challenging times. Perhaps you wish to become more wise or ferocious.

to Magical Resistance

1. Brainstorm a list of possibilities. You can think about your commitments (vows, spiritual guides, gods, ancestors), your beliefs, or qualities that are valuable to you.

2. Decide what materials to use. You could draw freehand, use a tablet, or even use drafting tools (I use these for sacred geometry work). Even when I plan to transfer my design to wood panel for a painting, I draw the image out a few times on paper with pencil in order to make corrections.

3. Decide what colors you will use (polychromatic or monochromatic). Will it be black & white?

4. Plan your background. Negative space is important to me because my masks have gaps to allow the abstract paintings underneath to show; thus, I tend to add masks to an already painted substrate. You could also leave the surface blank or decide after your mask has been finished, but it is effective to make that choice early in the process.

5. Begin with a basic shape: a circle, oval, square, or even triangle. Eyes are important to me, sometimes I draw them first and other times I will add them last. What features would you like to include? What details are unnecessary? Sometimes deciding what to omit is just as important as deciding what to keep. Will your mask be symmetrical or asymmetrical?

6. Continue the process: will you use your mask in performance or share the image? Is it just for meditation?

In conclusion, masks are an important part of history, religion, art, and culture, but they are not mere relics of the past. Despite the negative associations of forced hiding or treachery, we can excavate from mask iconography and practice something worthwhile for the present. Masks can help us reclaim power over ourselves and understand who we are as well as what is valuable to us. They can help us transform into people who can thrive in the future. They can help use see potential in difficult liminal spaces of disruption and change. When we feel trapped in a materialist and exploitative reality, the mask provides us with a door we can open if we choose.

REFERENCE

I.-M.B. Danielsson, *Masking moments: the transitions of bodies and beings in late iron age scandinavia* (dissertation), (Stockholms universitet, 2007).

to Magical Resistance

Heedless and Headless: The Witchcraft of Laverna
Thumper Forge

THE MOST WELL-KNOWN GODS in Charles Godfrey Leland's *Gospel of the Witches* are Diana, Lucifer, and of course Their daughter Aradia. However, towards the back of the book, Leland introduces readers to a more obscure deity: Laverna, the rascally Witch Goddess of thieves, plagiarists, and those who conceal their activities behind the cover of darkness.

And I *adore* Her, y'all. I mean, I try to be virtuous or whatever, but the fabric of my checkered past is spattered with libations to Laverna, whose watchful eyes and quick hands have gotten me out of more scrapes than I honestly care to consider.

We don't know much about Laverna's history—Leland is really the only author to provide comprehensive information about Her. But she does make a couple of appearances in ancient Roman literature, in which She was considered one of the *Di Inferni*: literally "the Gods below," chthonic spirits of the Underworld. And we also know that She had a sanctuary outside of Rome, where devotees would venerate Her in silence, making offerings with their left hands and praying that She'd assist them with whatever shady capers they were trying to pull off.

The tale Leland shares about Laverna—which he attributes to the poet Virgil—gives us insight into Her personality. Following is my bowdlerized version.

Once upon some time ago, Laverna targeted a wealthy priest and was like, "Hey, if you sell me all your land, I'll build a temple to our Gods. I swear on my body that I'll pay you in six months." The priest was like, "Okay, seems legit," and handed ownership of the property over to Laverna, who immediately flipped it and bailed on him.

She then zeroed in on a noble and was like, "I'd like to buy your castle, please. I swear on my head that I'll pay you in six months."

The Gorgon's Guide

The noble was all, "Nothing can go wrong with this amazing deal," and handed over the keys. But like she did with the priest, Laverna fenced everything and slipped away, stiffing the noble in the process.

At some point, the priest and the noble were introduced to each other—I assume at some sort of support group—and were like, "*We've been done wrong by a Goddess.*" When confronted by the rest of the Gods over Her actions, Laverna's body disappeared, which, as She pointed out, meant that the oath She swore to the priest was void. And when the Gods were like, "Um, you also swore on your head, hon," Her body reappeared *without* a head, and Her voice (now emanating from Her neck) was like, "What head, yo? *I have no head at all.*"

The Gods found the whole show entertaining as all get-out, and while They did make Her pay back the priest and the noble, They didn't impose any other sanctions on Her: Instead, They basically gave her a promotion, and announced that Laverna would be the Goddess of everyone who lives by deceit. Which is a good fit for Her. But, according to Leland, Laverna was also invoked by those who found themselves pregnant and, for whatever reason (their business, not mine) didn't want to have children, a fate from which Laverna was happy to spare them. As such, She is very much a Goddess of reproductive freedom.

Since the Supreme Court of the United States overturned *Roe v. Wade*, effectively making abortion a criminal offense in many areas of the country, Laverna is as important a Goddess now as she was when Virgil told stories about Her.

Everything I've ever read about Laverna suggests that She is to be entreated quietly, or in silence, with one notable exception. In *Aulularia* by the Roman playwright Plautus (254–184 BCE), a character whose possessions have been stolen loudly prays to Laverna to avenge him and punish the thief. Despite being a thief Herself, Laverna offers protection from thievery to those who call upon Her.

As those in positions of power work to steal liberty from the marginalized and oppressed, so can we pray to Laverna to keep our

to Magical Resistance

liberty from being stolen. When fascist lawmakers attempt to outlaw the existence of queer, trans, and non-binary people, we can invoke Laverna to back us up as we fight for our right to exist. And whenever we band together, in shadows or subcultural underworlds, we can draw courage and power from the knowledge that Laverna is watching over us.

Let's just remember that Laverna is a gleeful Goddess, and Her irreverence can (and should) be channeled into our actions. Here's an easy suggestion on how to start doing that.

A lot of us end our spells with "So Mote It Be," which, y'know, works: It's a phrase that carries authority and finality. But magic is about turning possibility into probability by bending the laws of reality. It's about getting things done in the liminal spaces outside of the mainstream, and conjuring change both without and within.

So the next time you're casting a spell in the name of magical resistance, and your ritual is coming to a close, think about Laverna, the Goddess of getting away with it. Meditate on how She changed in accordance with Her will, and how She evaded the established rules of engagement. Visualize your goal accomplished, despite every mundane obstacle stacked against it. Taste freedom in the back of your throat. And instead of saying "So Mote It Be," smile brilliantly and repeat the words of Laverna Herself:

"I have no head at all."

Your spell will succeed. Your magic will help. And somewhere out in the darkness, a Goddess will whisper, *"Hell, yes."*

The Apotropaic Power of Medusa's Blood
RED CORAL CHARM TO WARD OFF EVIL

Emiliano Russo

R ED CORAL. Its Latin name is *Corallium rubrum,* in reference to its bright red color, known to us also as precious coral. The word coral may derive from the Greek *koraillon,* meaning "hard skeleton" for others, however, from the Greek *kura-halos,* meaning "human form", and still others, finally, derive the term from the Hebrew *goral,* which indicated a set of stones used for oracular purposes in Asia Minor and the Mediterranean.

Whatever the origin of its name, for more than four thousand years, red coral has found wide use within magickal practice, witchcraft, folklore and has been connected to many deities within different cults. In Egypt it was sacred to Isis; in Rome to Venus; Goddess Thetis is often depicted with red coral in her hair while in more recent times it is an ornament of the Madonna to whom splendid coral rosary beads are dedicated. But the most interesting association, is the one that connects coral to the tragic story of Medusa. According to myth, in fact, coral is said to have been born from the blood of Medusa's head, beheaded by Perseus, as told by Ovid in his *Metamorphoses.* After cutting off the Gorgon's head, Perseus washed his hands in the sea, and the blood of the unfortunate Medusa settling on the sea plants turned them to stone and gave them their red color. Even today some aquatic plants are precisely called *"gorgonians."*

This deep and direct relation to the blood of the Gorgon is reflected in almost all the magickal and beneficial properties of red coral, which is transculturally considered a symbol of immortality, as in China. For Pliny the Elder, red coral had the power to prevent and stop nosebleeds. I think it is interesting to note that in fact the shape of precious coral is somewhat resembling that of the human circulatory system. Avicenna,

to Magical Resistance

the father of Medieval medicine, also knew this well, recommending it to *"cheer up the forces of the heart"*—in short, albeit very demurely, he recommends it as an aphrodisiac, a sort of Medieval Viagra!

Red coral was almost always used in powder form, and because of its association with blood, it is possible that at one point it was used in place of human sacrifices. In ancient Egypt, coral powder was scattered over fields to propitiate abundant harvests by keeping away frost and locusts and was used against women's infertility, becoming over time the quintessential amulet used by pregnant women, birthing women and infants, effective in preventing seizures, dog coughs, and teething pains. Even in Greek tradition, women used coral for physical beauty, to promote fertility and milk production. Beads, pinecones, acorns and other elements were added to it to increase its apotropaic properties.

The great physician Discorides in the first century AD speaks of red coral twigs as a panacea for the cure of all ills, while for the medical-philosopher Paracelsus, when manipulated by an expert, red coral was a *"medicine to be preferred to all the treasures of the world"*, and even today it is used in a wide array of pharmaceuticals.

Here in Italy, however, red coral is notorious for being and providing great protection, and it is no coincidence that one of the most powerful amulets in Italian Folk-Craft is a red coral horn, considered as much a good luck charm as a powerful protection that can petrify evil like Medusa's gaze.

Even today, the great power of red coral is still strongly felt in southern Italy, where superstitious observances still hold strong; in fact, they are so implanted on the ordinary customs as to constitute a major part of everyday life. Foremost among these superstitions, and perhaps the most deeply rooted of them all is the belief in the power of the Evil Eye, or, to use a more entirely Neapolitan expression, the *jattura*. *Jettatori,* or bringers of bad-luck, differ from a Witch who casts curses and hexes willingly, in that bad-luck may be brought on by them unconsciously, and without intentional malice. This evil influence may at any moment

The Gorgon's Guide

cast a spell on the unwary. A chance meeting with the *jettatore* when you are on business bent, will mar the issue of it; if he or she kindly wishes you "good-day," your day will be a series of misfortunes; their presence anywhere will produce accidents which will affect all present but themselves. In Naples, amulets intended to secure the wearer against the power of the *jettatore*, are to be procured at reasonable prices at the coral and tortoise-shell, silversmiths', and jewellers' shops, which are visited by rich and poor alike. In their show-cases may be seen rows of twisted pieces of coral hearts fashioned from bone, shell and coral, fists with fingers variously extended or doubled up, hunchbacked mannikins, pigs, nuts, trefoil, claws, horns, teeth, and many others.

A simple and powerful spell to ward off evil is to get a red coral horn and consecrate it in Medusa's name so that it petrifies negative energies. You could choose a pendant to wear around your neck in your everyday life or during meditations and travels to the Spirit Realms to move around safely. You can hang it on a threshold, in front of your doorway, on a window, on the rearview mirror of your car to protect your travels; under your pillow to protect your dreams and banish nightmares and psychic attacks during sleep. You could place a red coral horn inside a Witch Bottle or in a mojo bag for luck and protection. Traditionally, a red horn should be given to newborn babies or those moving into a new home. Are you unable to find a red coral horn or does the use of this item seem unethical for your practice? No problem, Italian Folk-Craft knows a viable substitute for the red coral horn: a red chili pepper horn!

to Magical Resistance

Transforming Anger Sigil
Laura Tempest Zakroff

BUILT INTO THIS SIGIL:

- ¶ Encouraging constructive growth vs. destructive action
- ¶ Space to be heard and acknowledged
- ¶ Providing resources and support
- ¶ Direction – disperse, dispels, or positively builds
- ¶ Cleansing
- ¶ Healing

WHAT TO DO WITH THIS SIGIL: Rather than directing anger and creating violence, this sigil transforms that energy so that the end result is more constructive and supportive. Place on candles with a focus towards areas of conflict and violence, where to demonstrations and other events that are susceptible to violence that may disrupt or hide the message.

Magick of/for the Fierce Hearts

Irisanya Moon

THE WORLD CRUMBLES AT THE EDGES and for a while, it was hard to see. I was content, happy even to be in the middle of privilege and in the midst of comfort—numb and willing to stay that way. It was easier. It was quiet. It was convenient. It was the type of life that would have been perfectly wonderful.

But the world crumbles. Structures are upended. Or need to be. More every day. Perhaps it's more like an unweaving of carefully spun wool, easily draped over eyes. The light breaking through, the truth becoming sharper.

I call to the fierceness of unraveling it all. I call to the heart that beats alongside terror and trembling. I call to the chambers and the tunnels that transport blood across a life. I call to:

SELF DEVOTION / CAST THE CIRCLE
The art of caring for the self in ways that expand beyond water and rest.

Igniting devotion to yourself builds a foundation of resilience and resource. What do you need to be well cared for? What do you need to bring in and let go of? What boundaries do you require to live in devotion to yourself and others? What nourishment do you need to prioritize? How can you gift yourself joy and pleasure? How can you lay within the temple of your body and heart, surrendering to your knowing to find strength and courage and trust and truth? There are difficult, hard choices to be made when you devote yourself fully to the precious being you are.

COMMUNION / DEEPEN INTO THE INTENTION & INVITE THE GODS
The practice of knowing and honoring something larger than you.

This is the place of devotion to the above and below, to the places of mystery. Some might call it divine. Some might call it moonlight. Staring deep into the eyes of that which exists beyond structure and form and logic makes room for creation. Finding a way to honor that which has always existed and will continue long after your last breath will place you in the wider story of fierceness. Will allow you to know yourself as part of something so much bigger than everyday worries and disagreements. (These will happen anyway.) What can you worship? What will you build an altar of intention to? What can you sit beside in the quiet moments of desperation and ask the questions that truly matter? What can you trust in the face of overwhelming oppression, corruption, and greed? What will you turn to when all else seems to fade away?

COMMUNITY / COME TOGETHER TO SEND THE MAGICK OFF
The dance of interdependence and the need for others.

I imagine us standing in the streets together, in the wide open field, in the ritual circle, in the quiet shadow of a half-opened door. Together. Engaged. Committed. Holding each other up. The structures of power may seek to place us into identities and roles, into the furthest corners away from your eyes and my eyes, but we will find each other. Build networks of aid and knowing. Who shares this world with you? What do you offer to each other? How can you be the ones you trust? How do these hands fit together? What might they make from the ashes that scatter from what needs to be burned?

OPEN THE CIRCLE / REVEAL YOUR FIERCE HEART

This is not a time for comfort or ease. You know this. I know this. We will know it again and again. Let us embrace and ignite our fierceness by devoting to self, devoting to mystery, and devoting to each other.

We do not do this work alone.

Cycle Breaker Sigil
Sidney Eileen

THE CYCLE BREAKER SIGIL is all about breaking free from toxic cycles and patterns, and getting out of ruts so we have the opportunity to build better futures for ourselves. This sigil can be applied on a personal level to help break bad habits or addictions, on an interpersonal level to break free of toxic relationship dynamics or generational trauma, on a societal level to break down structural violence and systemic oppression, or on any issues where the established cycles and patterns are damaging and seem unavoidable or unchangeable.

It uses both banishment and manifestation energy in balance to remove obstacles and create dramatic change even when it seems impossible to break free. It also encourages other people to leave the cycles by becoming more aware and either going with the changes you are instigating, or breaking free in their own direction.

If you are using the Cycle Breaker Sigil to address personal cycles or patterns, be prepared for the possibility that you will also need to do shadow work to address the root causes of your cycle or pattern. Addressing and healing root causes supports lasting change and helps prevent falling fully back into old cycles and patterns.

Shadow work may also be needed if you are using the Cycle Breaker Sigil for interpersonal cycles and patterns, to help heal the wounds that have kept you in toxic or damaging relationships, be they friendships, mentorships, family, generational trauma, or something else.

At the other end of the spectrum, the Cycle Breaker Sigil can be used to encourage increased awareness of social problems and tear down structural violence cycles and toxic cultural patterns. It can be added as a component to rituals and spellwork with social justice and social change in mind, or used in combination with other sigils that target specific problems. This won't necessarily involve shadow work, but the intention to recognize root sources can potentially create the need for shadow work to challenge internalized narratives, privileges, and behaviors that support the cycles and patterns you seek to break. Creating lasting change requires changing those patterns both externally and internally.

Symbology and Intentions

The main structure of the sigil is a broken infinity symbol, to indicate breaking free from what seem like immutable and everlasting problems.

¶ Awareness of toxic cycles and patterns. Before it is possible to make deliberate changes, you must first be aware that the problem exists. This is symbolized by the open eye, placed below the rest of the sigil to emphasize that awareness is the foundation of intentional, lasting change.

¶ Recognize root sources. Once you recognize a toxic cycle or pattern exists, the next step is to recognize the root sources which are causing that toxic cycle or pattern. Finding those root causes is symbolized by the pentagram at the top of the sigil, where it can see everything involved and create enlightened awareness.

¶ Strength to break from established cycles and patterns. It is not an easy thing to break free from established cycles and patterns, no matter the scale. Inertia matters, and most people will gravitate to the familiar, even if the familiar is harmful, because the unknown is scary. This strength is symbolized in the pentagram, providing support on all levels, and in the shattered infinity loop that shows it can be done.

The Gorgon's Guide

¶ Wards against falling back into old cycles and patterns. Making dramatic changes is never a straight road. It always involves unexpected changes of direction and setbacks. It is very normal to find yourself drawn back into old patterns and cycles, or having relapses. That does not mean you failed. It just means the job isn't finished yet, and more cycle breaking needs to happen. So, give yourself grace, have a rest if you need it, pick yourself up, and keep going. This is symbolized primarily by the broken infinity symbol, which in being broken cannot resume in exactly the way it did before, even if you dip back into that rut for a bit before completely escaping. It is also symbolized in the two shoots flying away from the cycle and disconnecting from it entirely, leaving the cycle in the past.

¶ Facilitate dramatic changes. By the time we are stuck in a rut, it is usually long past the point where small, incremental changes will do the trick. Instead, it is drastic and rapid change that is needed, because small changes will just get eaten in the established cycle and barely create a ripple. This is symbolized by the dramatic turn of each line before it shoots off entirely away from the rut.

¶ Encourage others to follow suit. It is important for other people to also see the root problems and take steps to both destroy toxic cycles and support beneficial changes. If you are using the Cycle Breaker Sigil on a personal level, this is important so those in your life can understand and support the changes you are making. On a relationship level, this is important so that other people in the relationship can also make beneficial changes and the relationship can grow instead of dying. On a social level, this is important because without mass awareness and action, we will not be able to create lasting changes. This is symbolized by the multiple arrows rushing to escape the cycle. They are flowing in two separate directions to indicate that not everyone who escapes a toxic cycle will go in the same direction. There are multiple arrows in each direction to indicate that when one person breaks a cycle, there are very often other people who will follow the new path as well after seeing what is possible.

To Bind the Cruel

Ivy Senna

THIS RITE could be used to bind a person of authority or an institution who abuses or harms others. On the night of the dark Moon, perform this prayer to Hekate, adapted from PGM IV.2785–2890:

Hail Hekate Ophioplokamos,
Nether, nocturnal, and infernal queen.
You who devour meals amid the graves,
You who drink blood, bringing death and destruction,
You who resound grief, feasting on hearts,
With scales of serpents you are dark,
With hair of serpents, coils of writhing snakes,
Flaming, serpent-girded mistress,
Dressed in snakes, O flesh-eating Drakaina!
Hail Goddess, and hear my call.
ARARACHARARA EPHTHISIKERE!
ARARACHARARA EPHTHISIKERE!
ARARACHARARA EPHTHISIKERE!

Then, burn an incense of myrrh as an offering to Hekate before continuing with the prayer.

I burn for you this myrrh,
Dart-shooter, heavenly one, goddess of harbors who roam the mountains, Goddess of crossroads, O nether and nocturnal, and infernal,
Goddess of dark, quiet and frightful one. Come to me, as Moira and Erinys,
As torment, as Justice and Destroyer.
Come to me, Queen-who-keeps-Kerberos-in-chains. Just as you keep

mighty Kerberos in chains,
Assist me in chaining [insert name of person or institution],
So that they will be unable to inflict harm upon others ever again.

Hekate of the Snakes, Hekate of the Chains,
May [insert name of person or institution] be ever chained!

With myrrh ink, write the name of the person or institution you wish to bind onto three strips of paper. Then, one by one, tie a knot around each strip of paper with a single cord of black rope. Thus, with the cord, will you form three knots with a name bound inside each of them. Additionally, some black dog fur can also be tied into the knot to add a potency to the rite.

Whilst tying each knot, say the following charm:

I knot the cord, I lock the chain, I bind you, [name of person or institution].

After that is done, pour an offering of red wine as a show of appreciation to the goddess. Bowls of fruit pits such as cherry pits can also be offered to the goddess as well.

Next, make your way to a cemetery and place three coins at the entranceway of the cemetery before entering. Then, approach a patch of graveyard ivy and offer it a glass of cool water as you say the following:

O Hedera Helix, Serpent of the Green, Lady of the Knotted Binds, I give you this offering of cool water.
In the name of Hekate of the Snakes, of Hekate of the Chains, I ask that you bind for me [name of person or institution].
Keep them restrained. Keep them in chains.
And as the corpses beneath this earth, Rot and decay,
So may their powers dwindle and wane.

to Magical Resistance

Then, say the following charm, adapted from Hymn VIII of the Atharvaveda:

Let them not be freed from the noose of misery.
Let them not be freed from the noose of disappearance.
Let them not be freed from the noose of the trees.
Let them not be freed from the noose of the shrubs.
Let them not be freed from the noose of the seasons.
Let them not be freed from the noose of the months.
Let them not be freed from the noose of day and night.
Let them not be freed from the noose of heaven and Earth.

Tie the knotted cord to the vine of the ivy, and depart without looking back.

Boldly Reclaiming "I am"
Nova Pax Thrasher

Around the 4th grade, I discovered poetry. I picked out a copy each of Robert Burns and Jewel at a wholesale/used bookstore housed in an old church, devouring the variation in voice. If I remember correctly, I preferred Jewel. This immediately led to attempting my own little verses, already a fan of the craft in general after having written a feminist story about Vikings in school. From then on you could not find me without my sticker-coated composition book.

One day, a boy took a peek at one I was working on, my precious book left open on a school desk. It was an affirmation-type piece beginning "I am cool, I am — " To be honest, I do not genuinely know any of the other adjectives I used, but that was the one he pointed to, the one that sticks in my memory like The Ghost of Embarrassments Past.

"No, you're not."

My heart sank.

I mean, I *knew* I wasn't popular, but the confrontation with reality was too much for my decade-young self. I did not stop writing, but I did stop talking about it.

Yet, that traumatic invasion of privacy and subsequent harsh criticism did not stop me from following my ultimate passion; my life now revolves around poetry when not otherwise obligated... and often *when* otherwise obligated. The journey from "uncool" 4th grader to "arguably badass" poet was not without further setbacks. I denied myself the joy off and on, or life was too hard, or I didn't have time, or... I had to face it at some point: my only option was to embrace my ~~obsession~~ gift and write furiously.

However, it was not until I claimed my space that the holy audacity took over. That is what I call this bold claim of sacred inversion: holy audacity. I had to take those words spoken, that curse, and break it by

to Magical Resistance

perverting the lies. Instead of living in shame, I have given myself permission to be seen—as I am—whole and unrefined.

I call this boldness "holy" because I believe it is a gift from the gods, ancestors, and nature spirits I work with. Some days the impudent risks are only possible because something outside myself has spurred me into action, contemplation, or revision. "Audacity" is a somewhat ambiguous word containing multi-faceted definitions, with Oxford saying it is both "a willingness to take bold risks" and "rude or disrespectful behavior; impudence." I cannot help but wonder who gets to decide what is "bold" versus "impudent," if there is discretion in blame or praise?

There are many people who would like to see me silent for various reasons. Maybe not me in particular, although a few of those probably exist, but for who I am. I am non-binary and queer. I am mentally ill. I am a witch. I am a poet. To empower myself, to find and strengthen my voice, those identities must be celebrated… even if I am the one to light the candle, even if the numina is "all" that cheers me on.

Now, after my journey, I read my poems at bars and make chapbooks by hand with a giant stapler. I write constantly and with immense passion, a zest for life bleeding on the page. Now *I am*.

And I am not always worried about the adjective that comes next.

Writing may not be your thing. It isn't everyone's. But there is probably an authentic part of yourself, a talent or quality, that you are denying while it simply yearns to nourish you. It is probably a shame-type thing. I swear, so much pain comes from wounds of shame. Investigate. Sit with it/them. Then claim your space, your title, your name and place in the world. Introduce yourself to the stars as "I am."

Use this spell when the bastards get you down and you need to remind them, and yourself, who you are.

The Gorgon's Guide

☞ INGREDIENTS:

¶ Candle in your favorite color or one you associate with confidence and power

¶ Mirror

¶ Pen

¶ Paper

¶ Lighter/matches/etc.

¶ Thing to put fire in

Open Sacred Space of your choice.

When settled, light your candle while invoking a deity/ancestor/spirit close to you and who you believe wants to see your confidence grow. With this companion invoked, write "I am" on a piece of paper. Feel free to add an adjective. Feel free not to.

While looking in the mirror (if that is comfortable for you; I personally have issues looking in the mirror sometimes—or use this spell to challenge yourself!), speak or mentally recite the prayer on the facing page. Do this as many times as feels right. Improvise if you come up with something personal.

When ready, light the paper with the candle, and let it burn *(insert Fire Safety 101)*. Focus on releasing shame and igniting an audacious authenticity as you watch the flames. This is both death and rebirth, so let the liminal sing in your magic. Hold the discomfort, then let it go. Find your Happy Medium.

When you feel ready, thank the deity/ancestor/spirit you invoked earlier and close Sacred Space.

Keep the ashes and use them in related spell work, scatter near an important place, or whatever feels right regarding keeping/saying goodbye to this ritual.

to Magical Resistance

*I am fire
I am wind
I am a force to be reckoned with
I am death
I am rebirth
I am putting myself first
I am water
I am healing
I am more than entrapment in feeling
I am reason
I am love
I am filled with wisdom from above
I am whole
I am filled
I am the embodiment of my will
I am new
I am pure
I am making my footing sure
I am learning
I am growing
I am rooted and it is showing
I am steadfast
I am bold
I am proud to be getting old
I am truth
I am desire
I am choosing to aim higher*

Shadow Work with Snake Energy
THE GORGON'S MASK, SHAME, AND SELF-EMPOWERMENT

Joey Morris

Scales in the void, the eternal ellipsis of rebirth, vilified, demonized and feared. Lidless eyes peer into the depths of our souls and we, as humans, flinch at the "otherness."

IN TIMES LONG PAST, the sand and earth parted as the side-winding symbol of deeply connective Goddess energy imparted wisdom to those willing to learn. The snake symbolized fertility, healing, sexual liberation, and rebirth. But as a culture of sexual repression and shame rose up in the dregs of history, the once revered snake became cursed. In Genesis 3.14, we read, "*Cursed are you above all livestock and wild animals. You will crawl on your belly and you will eat dust all the days of your life!*"

In modern times, the spiritual significance of the serpent and the wisdom to be found within its mask are complicated and fundamentally individual, based on the perspective of one's spiritual leanings and the degree to which one has internalised biased teachings and propaganda.

Some modern witch culture embraces snake energy, although unfortunately it often falls within a perception of the so-called "dark" witch iconography, still being associated with the "evil" witch, such as in the film *The Craft* (1996), when Nancy says, "*The Serpent is a very powerful being. You should respect it.*"

Within popular consciousness, disassociating the snake from its biblical damnation is nearly impossible, even when, as pagans, we seek to reject dogmatic overtures. It sneaks up on us in popular culture that portrays the snake as "deceiver." The snake, once synonymous with healing, represented even now through the staff of Asclepius, is simultaneously used as a term for false medicine—"snake-oil."

"A snake in the grass" refers to someone who means you harm and is lurking and waiting to strike. The entire inner physiology of the snake's mouth has negative connotations. A forked tongue (which aids a snake's sense of smell) has been vilified into a synonym for "liar," and a mouth full of venom may be a snake's mechanism for defense (or hunting) but has been adopted by humans to indicate a hateful and slanderous gossip.

So, when we as spiritual practitioners approach the mask of the serpent, we ultimately find ourselves as equally keen to place its cool scales against our skin in order to breathe in its lidless lessons as we are hesitant, influenced by notions that we may be led astray, down a path of deception and lies. Some even approach the energy of the snake with a desire to become more poisonous and venomous in themselves, believing power lies in such involvement.

The mask of the snake reveals itself to be just as complex as trying to discern the truth about snake energy. The mask contains as many mirrors within it as the serpent has scales, revealing a multitude of lessons depending on where the witch wishes to delve. *For me, the magic of the Serpent began with addressing the tangled shadow lesson of dealing with internalised shame.*

Shame is the conflict within the snake medicine of personal transformation and personal (often sexual) liberation, for shame is akin to a nail that hammers down the process of shedding one's outmoded skin. Personal evolution begins with a sense of self-worth, that we can be deserving of the process. Nowhere is this more painfully obvious than within the Greek mythology centred around Athena and her priestess, Medusa.

The very name Medusa hints at the nature of the truth behind this myth, which has been perverted by that same repressive agenda that has dogged history. Medusa is from the Greek word *Medousa*, which means "guardian." which stems from the verb, *medein*: "to protect, rule over." (See etymonline.com).

Additionally, Medusa was often depicted as physically beautiful, which in patriarchal Greek mythology traditionally ends badly for mortals encountering Gods. In Ovid's *Metamorphoses*, we read:

> Medusa once had charms; to gain her Love
> A rival crowd of envious lovers strove.
> They, who have seen her, own, they ne'er did trace
> More moving features in a sweeter face.
> Yet above all, her length of hair, they own,
> In golden ringlets wav'd, and graceful shone.

Ovid also describes how Medusa had dedicated herself as a virgin priestess to the goddess Athena, and was subsequently raped by Poseidon, defiling her and the temple. This account then attributes Athena as wrathful, further "punishing" Medusa for this "offence," and transforming her once golden curls into venomous snakes. Medusa became a scaled serpentine monster.

The shadow energy of shame and the symbolism of snakes is unmistakable here. While the myth suggests that Athena felt shamed by the defilement of her priestess and temple, and further shamed the victim of the attack as a result, this does not seem in keeping with a few key points of Athena's mythos. Athena is referred to as "La Serpentine" in other works of Orphic poetry, one of her most dedicated followers was associated with snakes, and she wore the Gorgon head on her shield—a key line of personal defense in battle.

Could it then not be possible that instead, a subversion of myth has taken place, bent on shaming female figures of empowerment so that these once serpentine gifts of solidarity became indicative of resentful wrath? Through a distortion in story-telling, a shadow of shame crept in, aimed to condition and polarize people by gender, and particularly to vilify any independent or dominant woman, free of the constraint of expected patriarchal rule—to transform those goddesses or "guardians" into monsters.

The demonization of both Athena and her priestess Medusa seems indicative of the patriarchal influence within Hellenistic society. Athena is described as non-sexual and warlike, both attributes that go against

to Magical Resistance

accepted Greek norms for female roles, and so she is rendered into a spiteful, heartless goddess by the myth, rejecting another woman who is faced with the ultimate act of violent disempowerment. Medusa, disavowing her beauty to become a virginal priestess of Athena (and thus denying those "envious lovers") is raped by the god that Athena bested in fair contest; thus Poseidon seeks to shame Athena for her victory and shame her priestess.

But Poseidon's actions do not overturn Athena's victory at Athens, and Medusa's physical transformation by Athena is actually a gift that frees her from the cage of physical appearance and bestows supernatural abilities upon her.

Of course, liberated women in myth do not stay that way for long. Perseus claims masculine victory over Medusa using his shield as a "mirror" to murder her with her own power. He thus forces the notion of a woman's physical appearance being of tantamount importance. Confronted by her non-conformity to traditional standards of beauty, Medusa turns herself to stone.

Medusa continues to be honoured by Athena however who carries the Gorgon head shield into battle and gifts Asclepius with two drops of her blood; one cures all sickness and even resurrects people, and the other is a deadly poison. Thus the legacy and magic of the snake (death and rebirth) was passed on through a modern magical art, that of healing.

The shadow of shame perpetuated by societal control still rears its head to this day. The mythology of Medusa, in being retold for every generation, is not forgotten. Yet the energy of the snake continues to evolve, and Medusa has become for many an icon of female rejection of standardized beauty and uniformity.

The snake mask invites us to learn these lessons for ourselves. Shame may be a weapon of choice for those seeking to control us, but it cannot break the spirit of self-empowerment, which will always resurrect. The connection between all people is an energy akin to the scales on the back of the Ouroboros.

Flower Essences for Spiritual Activation
Lindsey Pszwaro

YARROW, BLACK-EYED SUSAN, AND MILKWEED flower essences are vibrational medicines and tools to take you through the underworld and back again. Protect yourself, enter the shadow, and then rise with divine energy to create the world you seek. The medicine we need blooms when we need it most. Here are three flower essence teachings and their indications, along with a general recipe for making flower essences.

Flower essences are made from fresh flowers steeped directly in pure water and sunlight. They capture the energetic signature (or vibration) of a plant and therefore work on an energetic and emotional level. As medicine, flower essences daily nudge you into a higher vibration. This gentle preparation is a powerful soul medicine during these times of transition.

YARROW: BOUNDARIES AND PROTECTION

Flower essence indications — provides physical, emotional and spiritual boundaries and protection; helps in maintaining integrity despite difficult circumstances; emotional strength and courage.

Yarrow has a delicate yet strong beauty. Sweet individual blossoms make up a shield shape. Together, unified and protected, they are an umbrella or umbellifer plant: a true warrior plant. Most roadside herbs are considered warriors, as they protect the boundaries of the wild.

Yarrow has been revered by ancient cultures as a protective herb. The ancients recognized its alchemical blending of strength and sensitivity. Yarrow, or *Achillea millefolium*, was named for Achilles, who had to protect his one vulnerable spot. Yarrow is indeed a "vulnerary" herb, used for wounds, to slow and stop bleeding. It makes sense that we use

to Magical Resistance

the Yarrow flower essence for ways in which we feel "vulnerable" or "bleeding out" to the energies of others or to our environment. Yarrow allows us to remain sensitive and open, yet maintain the integrity of our healthy boundaries.

This essence can be taken as a daily tonic or as needed before entering an emotionally challenging situation, or to prevent getting drained by others' emotions.

BLACK-EYED SUSAN: SHADOW QUEEN

Flower essence indications — allows greater expansion, compassion and humility in going inward, locating your own shadow and excavating it. Black-Eyed Susan brings suppressed memories, ideologies or thoughts into awareness.

She is the deep, dark central eye with the golden crown. Black-Eyed Susan flower essence is a Shadow Queen. It is used when you are ready to dive into your shadow-work and look at what needs to be resolved. It allows you to connect with the pain: feel it to heal it.

Black-Eyed Susan is a portal that unlocks repressed emotions which may be stored in the subconscious mind or habitual body. It clears channels and gives you courage to move forward, outward and upward. The golden crown symbolizes it's holiness. It is about shedding away the darkness to bring about light. When paired with journaling, meditation or dream work, this flower essence is a powerful soul healer.

MILKWEED: DIVINE CREATION

Flower essence indications — supports bringing our creative and divinely inspired ideas into form. Honor what you create.

Milkweed connects you to Spirit and channels your inner work. It nurtures our will forces to persevere, rise above states of helplessness, and realize our inner spiritual power. Milkweed reminds you that you are an extension of the Divine. Your creation is the creation of the Divine.

Milkweed supports us in the necessary actions we need to translate our creative ideas into reality. It helps us remain confident in our vision, even in the face of opposition, so we can stay true to our dreams.

HOW TO MAKE FLOWER ESSENCES

INGREDIENTS:

Fresh flowers (be sure they haven't been treated with herbicide or pesticides)

1 cup Purified water

1 cup Brandy

Glass bowl

STEPS:

1. Fill glass bowl with 1 cup of purified water.

2. Harvest enough flower heads to cover the surface of the water. Shake off debris or insects and float them directly in the bowl.

3. Place bowl in direct sunlight for at least 4 hours or more.

4. Strain off water into a jar.

5. Add 1 cup brandy into jar to preserve.

6. Label jar with flower essence type and date. (Can be stored up to 6 years).

7. Funnel into smaller dropper bottles (*optional*)

REGULAR DOSAGE:

2-3 drops about 3 times a day.

A Sigil for the Protection of Transgender Rights

Laura Tempest Zakroff

BUILT INTO THIS SIGIL:

- Promote understanding
- Command respect, positive attention
- Increase compassion
- Opportunity for education
- Strength
- Foster Equality
- Build acceptance
- Lend protection

WHAT TO DO WITH THIS SIGIL: Similar to the Transfolx sigil, this sigil is focused on rights and legislation. These sigils can be used together or separately. You can wear it, share it, draw it in appropriate places, use it in places where rights are being violated or in danger, use it in postcards, legislation, and other material to educate folks. It's a front-line sigil for helping to defend trans rights, which are human rights.

A Sigil to Defend Transfolx

Laura Tempest Zakroff

BUILT INTO THIS SIGIL:

- ⁋ Protect transfolx
- ⁋ Stand up for them
- ⁋ Speak up to defend them
- ⁋ Help educate the world
- ⁋ Bring greater comprehension, understanding, empathy
- ⁋ Foster inclusion
- ⁋ Aid in healing

WHAT TO DO WITH THIS SIGIL: This sigil is focused to protect and defend the bodies and rights of transfolx You can wear it, share it, draw it in appropriate places, use it for blessings, tattoo it, etc. It can be used to defend one's home, body, or community place.

Invocation of the Outlander

M. Belanger

LONG BEFORE THE *Contendings of Horus and Set,* before the lamentable conflation with the Greek serpent Typhon, the Egyptian god Set was the only deity who possessed the strength and the courage to overcome the great serpent Apophis. As the boat carrying the vulnerable sun god descended into the underworld during the nightly hours, Set stood watch at the prow and fought off those forces determined to devour the light.

Set, whose color is red like the harsh deserts beyond the life-giving floods of the Nile. Set, whose metal is iron—but not just any iron. Meteoric iron. Literally star-stuff from beyond the bounds of what we recognize as home.

Although he was minimized and demonized to become the jealous sibling of Osiris, the creepy uncle of the infant Horus, long before that, Set was a twin. Old images depict him standing across from another falcon-headed Horus, each with their hands on a rope controlling a pillar which is arguably the *axis mundi*, the pivot-point of power, of time, of reality itself. The twins stood, equal and opposite forces, each indispensable to the balance of existence as we know it.

In that older worldview, outsiders like Set nevertheless held power. They occupied as important a place in the fabric of society as those embraced by more traditional structures.

Set, the god of the waste-places. Set the god of outcasts and foreigners. Set whose sexual expression was anything but heteronormative, who was arguably intersex and/or trans, and who has always stood for the powers and people who exist beyond the bounds.

It is to this Set—this older, wilder, radically inclusive force—this prayer is spoken. If you can, when you need a little strength in the face of those who would oppress you, step out at night, find the stars of the Big Dipper, and speak these words to the sky:

The Gorgon's Guide

Under the light of the Foreleg,*
In the silence of deep night,
I invoke thee, Patron of Outcasts,
Lord of the Red Lands.
Earth-shaker, Storm-maker,
Walker of boundaries
And what lies beyond.

IA Set!
Great-of-Strength, we call you:
Lift your star-forged iron
And slay the chaos
That threatens to swallow us.

Protect us,
your misfit children
who live and love and craft and speak
in places we're told we can't.
Be our comfort in this world
that rejects us
that passes laws to eject us.
Stand before us
behind us
beside us
and help us face down
those who would deny us our right to exist.

*The Big Dipper. In Egyptian astronomy, this is not a bear but part of a bull, and it has long-standing associations with the Great God Set. See "The Symbolism of the Foreleg Amputation in Ancient Egypt as an Offering" by M.H.M.A. Alrahman in the *Journal of the Faculty of Tourism and Hotels-University of Sadat City* 4.2/1 (Dec. 2020).

to Magical Resistance

Opening Hearts Ritual

Fr. Sean Wilde UE

I WAS INSPIRED TO WRITE THIS RITUAL on July 1, 2022, after watching various practitioners openly celebrating Canada Day, despite Canada's treatment of Indigenous people both historically and today. The idea is to open the hearts and minds of people to hear the trauma of marginalized people, the concerns of marginalized people and to be receptive to their message. Adapting this ritual to suit you is encouraged.

REQUIRED MATERIALS

- Five green candles (white will do if you cannot find green)
- Matches/lighter
- Five keys
- Road opening Incense
- Opening doors oil (olive oil will do if necessary)
- Cup of water
- A food you like, something like a cake, bread, or a pastry
- Small plate for the food

PREPARATION AND SET-UP

Cleanse each item.
Anoint each candle with the oil.
Place the candles in a pentagram configuration. It will need to be
    large enough for you to stand in the middle of it.
Beside each candle, place a key.
Place the plate at the north area of the pentagram, five inches away

from the top of the pentagram. Place the food on the plate and the cup of water beside it.

Light the incense, which should be near the pentagram.

Cast a circle in whatever way works for you. The circle must extend beyond the pentagram and objects.

Light each candle beginning with the top one and proceeding clockwise until all are lit.

Stand in the middle of the pentagram.

Turn to the East and call the quarter in the way you are familiar with.

Turn to the South and call the quarter in your way.

Turn to the West and call the quarter in your way.

Turn to the North and call the quarter in your way.

Call spirit in the way you are familiar with.

THE RITUAL

[Begin by facing North after calling the quarters and spirit]

I am [*name*].

Perform the invoking/activation pentagram for spirit.

I call upon the element and beings of spirit to assist me in my working today.

Turn to the East.

Perform the invoking/activation pentagram for air.

I call upon the element and beings of air to assist me in my working today.

Turn to the South.

Perform the invoking/activation pentagram for fire.

I call upon the element and beings of fire to assist me in my working today.

Turn to the West.

Perform the invoking/activation pentagram for water.

to Magical Resistance

I call upon the element and beings of water to assist me in my working today.

Turn to the North.

Perform the invoking/activation pentagram for earth.

I call upon the element and beings of earth to assist me in my working today.

You are all needed to assist me in my working today.

Open the hearts of others, that they may feel what is needed.

Open the ears of others, that they may hear what is needed.

Open the eyes of others, that they may see what is needed.

Open the mouths of others, that they may speak what is needed.

Element and beings of Spirit, assist me so others may receive this working.

Element and beings of Air, carry this message, so others may receive this working.

Element and beings of Fire, destroy any barriers to this message, so others may receive this working.

Element and beings of Earth, build a foundation for this message, so others may receive this working.

Element and beings of Water, ensure this message is remembered, so others may receive this working.

As I have spoken it, so shall it be.

Conclusion

Consume the water and food with intention, that your working be carried, received, and remembered as you eat and drink. After a brief period of time, you can snuff out the candles and the incense.

Citadel of Stone, Roots, and Ivy

Gwynevere Kipling

Queering the lived experiences of the now is a return to the primordial and unstructured chaos that Was, before the structures and rigid limitations of time, of day, and of role reinforced by a society of tick-boxes and imposition. Writing this part-essay part-poem part-call to a dream while working widdershins is an example of a small step that aligns just a little more to the off-kilter. Whether you are of the binary or immersed across the ways of being, whether you are within a lived experience where the definition is your own and deeply rooted or still discovering, finding moments to nestle within the strange and contrary is to build a wall within—a citadel of stone, of ivy, of hedge, and gorse.

> *Deep, raw wounds scored into crumbling dirt-flesh left barren.*
> *Gouging through roots, through vine, through aged wood.*
> *Laying bare the resting, the hidden, the vulnerable, the nurturing.*
> *The resting predator, the hiding prey, the restless scavenger,*
> *All made equal by humanity's thirst for faster, for more,*
> *For breaking the land to their will rather than adapting to it,*
> *Evolving with it, loving it, and attuning to its steady ways.*

Welcome serpents into it and your workings—skin-sloughing shifters of beguiling primality. Destruction—of the sacred self, of precious free time, of the ability to create, to delight, to enjoy the world as it should be—seems to be a relentless marching bulldozer. But for every act of horrific sundering must be a step taken to rewild and to heal. To recharge and to act in what ways are within your bounds. Whether it is helping a stranger, rescuing an animal in need, or even something so small as picking up litter that has blown into your path, it is the small actions that build the resilience. Every interlink build from a genuine seed

to Magical Resistance

of fighting for the preservation of what lies in contrast to More-Faster-Better is a bite, a snap, a snarl of your own making—whether it is turning creative outlets into beacons of awareness to decisions that can be made in consumption and what is supported, the ways of resistance are not always loud and bold. Do not feel disheartened if your resistance is not like anothers, for you are you—and whether your resistance is living or doing, acting, or conserving, the smallest quiet steps can show a fortitude of stone.

> *The longing within to rise, to shatter the machines of destruction,*
> *Resonating deep within under the ground.*
> *The presence in the air cloying with resin-thick blood.*
> *Ancient timbers strewn asunder, cast aside and their stories forgotten.*
> *Their wisdom discarded, the comfort they provide irrelevant in the face of profit.*

The land remembers and the land will not forgive. Humanity's destruction if kept on the course onto which it is driving down is not within the consideration of ancient nurtured liminal spaces and groves, of meadows and desolate abandoned places of settlement long since lost and taken back, hidden, and destroyed to become What Was once again.

> *Dirt-moistening weeping as safe dens and burrows are rent open.*
> *Shrubbery and shelter hauled into disarrayed piles.*
> *The sacred boundaries of hedge and shrub made broken branches and fuel-clogged leaves.*

Whether you are the bone-wielding stabber of iron into sheets of lead, snarling anger into the depths of the darkest places or the mourner of the lost who have no voice, the serpent cyclical Sees.

Wild sorbus and aged oak—deep, old, entrenched in the spirit of the land.
Protective ash, divine sycamore and the gentle willow, the silent comforters of those who walk softly under the shelter of their leaves.
Destroyed for speed, for convenience, for hollow achievement.

Gone will be the rich, untainted soils.
Gone will be the safe roosts of night-time foragers.
Gone will be an area of unfettered wildness.
Replaced by unfeeling steel, desolate iron and cold, broken stone.
Convenience forced from a perpetual wound on the landscape.

Just as it is important to shout and to fight is it important to lament and to remember. There needs to always be those who recall the older patterns within their before-memories. There is a need for the fighters and the front-of-the-line actors but there also need to be the storytellers, the healers, the helpers. There is a need for the lone watchers of the liminal places who step within and amidst that which is seen of as decay to all the better transgress against the impositions of Structure and Individual. There is a need for those who interlink aiding and aid-seeking, the daylight dancers and beacons of optimism and hope.

To fight against the destruction and loss doesn't always take a fighter with sword in hand. Resistance can be in the forging and forming of deepest roots that grow, that upend, that break through the cement, and tar.

to Magical Resistance

Deep Green Witchcraft and the Spirits of Place
Dodie Graham McKay

Do you believe that the world around you is alive with spirits?
I am a witch and an animist. That is to say that I believe that within all forms of life and landscape there are spirits and the potential to form constructive and mutually beneficial relationships with these spirits. I also believe that for these relationships to be effective, they must be reciprocal. In order to receive what I need and want from my environment; I must give something back.

In witchcraft we often draw upon the energy of our world to empower our magic. We raise energy from the natural forces around us, we call to the spirits in our environment to aid us in our work. We ask for luck and success in the physical world—for wealth and gain, for our own health and well-being and for political causes that benefit us.

We are human and rely on our planet to survive, in our mundane lives as well as our magical practices. How often do we consider what this relationship looks like from the perspective of the land and the spirits who dwell within it? Are we behaving in a way that inspires these spirits to aid us?

PEOPLE ARE PART OF THE LAND

It is a failing of western culture that we humans have divorced ourselves from an intimate connection to the land. Making this worse is that colonial cultures do not respect the remaining Indigenous cultures who are fighting to retain their own profound connections.

According to Amnesty International there are 370 million Indigenous people in approximately 90 countries worldwide.[1] It is common in these countries that Indigenous folks face discrimination, extremely high rates of poverty, threats to their cultures and identity, as well as loss of ancestral lands. The special and also spiritual relationship that

Indigenous peoples have formed with their lands over millennia binds their identities to the Earth.

If we truly are magical practitioners who see the world as alive and infused with spirit, we need to consider that these spirit beings may be more inclined to aid us if we treat the people with whom they have historically had relationships with dignity and respect.

You can choose to live your life and work your magic in a way that shows the land and the spirits that you are their ally to their people.

THINGS TO DO:

1. Educate yourself about who the original people of your area are. A good place to start is an interactive website called Native Land (https://native-land.ca/). This website features an interactive map that you can use to learn about the cultures, languages, and land rights of the Indigenous people in your part of the world.

2. Familiarize yourself with the United Nations Declaration on the Rights of Indigenous Peoples. Adopted by the United Nations in 2007, after decades of discussion and negotiations between Indigenous peoples and governments around the world, this document conveys "the rights of indigenous peoples in international law and policy, containing minimum standards for the recognition, protection and promotion of these rights. It establishes a universal framework of minimum standards for the survival, dignity, wellbeing and rights of the world's indigenous peoples."[2] It can be downloaded as a PDF at: https://www.ohchr.org/en/indigenous-peoples/un-declaration-rights-indigenous-peoples

3. Write a Land Acknowledgement Statement. In some parts of the world, such as Canada, Australia, and increasingly in the United States, a Land Acknowledgement is read at the beginning of an official public event or gathering. Throughout the neopagan world, people are beginning to use these statements as a way of expressing respect for Indigenous peoples and the land that we now share. The statement does not have to be long, but it must be carefully thought out and sincere,

to Magical Resistance

expressing your intent to support Indigenous people and do real work toward a better future.

SOME WRITING TIPS:

Learn the names of the Indigenous groups in your area and how to spell and pronounce them correctly. Open the statement by identifying that you are standing on their ancestral homeland.

Examine your motives for writing this statement. Do you have a genuine concern for the people and land you are speaking about?

Consider the context in which this statement will be spoken. If this will be used at the beginning of a public or private ritual, remember that what you say in sacred space may be heard by not only your human companions, but by the spirits that may be attracted to your magic as well.

Remember that a Land Acknowledgement Statement is empty and hollow without a commitment to affecting real-world change. Express a genuine gratitude and a commitment to justice and the betterment of Indigenous peoples and the land.

As an example, here is a Land Acknowledgement that I wrote for my coven to use at the very beginning of our rituals:

We stand now on Treaty One Territory, the ancestral land of the Anishinaabeg, Cree, Dakota, Dene, and Oji-Cree people, and the homeland of the Métis Nation. We give thanks to the land and people of Shoal Lake 40 First Nation for the gift of clean water. Before we invite the deities and elemental spirits of our tradition to this circle, we wish to show our respect to the spirits of this land, and assure them that we meet with peace, friendship, and a commitment to ongoing healing, justice, and reconciliation with the traditional people of this land.

Magic works on many levels, seen and unseen. What we do with our time and energy in our daily lives will have an impact on our magical lives as well. How we treat other people will be witnessed by the forces of nature that may also then choose to empower our magic.

NOTES

1. Amnesty International. "Indigenous People" accessed July 24, 2022 https://www.amnesty.org/en/what-we-do/indigenous-peoples/
2. United Nations. "UN Declaration on the Rights of Indigenous Peoples" accessed July 24, 2022 https://www.ohchr.org/en/indigenous-peoples/un-declaration-rights-indigenous-peoples

Three Workings for Protection
Estara Sanatani

BEGINNER: ROSES AND THORNS

You can do this spell entirely in your head. 🪻 Imagine two bubbles: one around the person you want to protect, and one around the person you want them protected *from*. Both are made of roses and thorns, with just this difference: for the person you're protecting, the roses are on the inside and the thorns are on the outside. For the person you're protecting them from, it's the reverse, roses on the outside and thorns on the inside. That's it!

Here's how it works. Let's say we're protecting Pat from Alex. Whenever Alex tries to be aggressive toward Pat, that energy is converted from the thorns they intend into roses, rendering them harmless. This effect is echoed by Pat's shield, which takes anything thorny aimed at Pat and turns it into flowers. Bad into good, presto! If someone tries to help Alex get around this block, no worries—anything intended to help Alex goes through in the other direction and gets turned into thorns. Is Pat vulnerable to being overly forgiving of Alex and contributing to their own abuse or oppression? Same thing—those inappropriate roses will never reach Alex.

Don't underestimate this one because it's simple.

INTERMEDIATE: FIVE PINS

Usually I go to this one when I'm blocking sexually inappropriate behavior. The five pins represent that. 🪻 YOU NEED: a votive candle, an anointing oil—something protective or good for your exact purpose, or else just plain olive oil—and five straight pins.

Anoint the candle with oil and think about binding the inappropriate behavior so it can no longer hurt anyone. If you work with deities

The Gorgon's Guide

or other helpful spirits, present your case to one you think will sympathize with your goal. (I go with Artemis for this particular spell.) When you've got your focus where you want it, stick the five pins into the votive candle at different heights.

Light the candle and watch it burn. You need to be attentive here, but it won't take too long—just use the time to keep putting forward your case and focusing on your goal. Watch for when the candle has melted enough that *one* pin falls out. When that happens, put out the candle. Five has become four: the sexual energy has become bound. You can keep the candle with its four pins in a safe place, bury it, or throw it out with other unwanted garbage.

ADVANCED: BOUND AND CIRCLED

This complex spell means you need more supplies and space, but it lets you add a lot of nuance.

⇨ YOU WILL NEED:

- A figure candle to represent the person(s) you are acting against

- Red string in a natural material (you'll be burning it)

- A plate on which to burn the figure candle

- An oil representing what you want to happen to the target (binding, hexing, passion cooling, etc.)

- *Optional*: a powder or salt representing what you want to happen to the target (doesn't have to be identical to the oil! You can use this to fine-tune the details)

- Four white pillar candles or 7-day candles

- A purification, protection, and/or justice oil

- *Optional*: a purification, protection, and/or justice powder or salt mix

to Magical Resistance

A NOTE ON THE WHITE CANDLES: you will be placing these around the image candle in the center. Things can get very interesting if you use pillars or tapers and put them too close to the center candle! You might want that, if you're going to watch it carefully. If not, you can avoid the issue by using 7-day candles.

Begin by naming the figure candle. Etch the name(s) into the wax, and then anoint it with the target oil. Take pieces of red string and bind the figure in the ways you want it bound: eyes to keep it from seeing or seeking, legs to keep it from approaching, arms to keep it from acting or touching, mouth to keep it from speaking, genitals to keep it from making sexual overtures, etc. If you're working with powders, sprinkle a bit of the target powder onto your plate and stand the figure candle in it.

Next, anoint the four white candles. These are your protection from any splashback, returns, or other unwanted consequences. They also function as an extra shield, blocking the target. Anoint them with your purification, protection, and/or justice oil, and place them around the figure candle. About nine inches to a foot away is good. If you have a powder to go with this part, sprinkle it around between the white candles to make a circle. Light the white candles first, then the figure candle in the center, and if possible let them burn all the way down. If you have to break this part into multiple sessions, always light the figure last and put it out first, so that the protective ring is always active while it's burning.

> I have used all three of these spells multiple times and
> they have been very effective every time.
> May they serve you well.

Reclaiming Power
AN APPLE CHARM
M. Belanger

I WROTE THIS SPELL originally for people recovering from toxic relationships. There are a lot of cord-cutting techniques out there, but so many focus only on the person or force being removed. This spell - which can be expanded to a small group ritual - is not merely a cutting away. It includes a potent act of reclaiming our own power. To me, that's an essential follow-up step.

We have relationships with many people and things through the course of our lives, and some of the most toxic grow out of unequal power dynamics. This spell is in no way limited to only the severing of romantic entanglements. Consider how we must cut away the influence of problematic family members, controlling bosses, culturally-ingrained biases, powerlessness imposed by authoritarian structures. In all of these cases, we have things we need to release and things we need to reclaim in order to recover our strength and be whole.

This is one way to do that.

For this spell, ☞ YOU WILL NEED ¶ an apple, ¶ a small paring knife, ¶ a larger, (ideally sharp) knife, and ¶ a cutting board. You will be eating the fruit, so if you don't like apples or cannot eat them for any reason, substitute a similarly sized, ideally round, edible object which has a soft enough surface for you to inscribe a couple words. You also need to be able to cut it in half.

Your first step is to distill your intent into two clear and personally significant words. Who or what are you cutting out of your life? What power are you reclaiming for yourself? While you may settle on short phrases, single, impactful words typically work best. Alternately, you may create two unique sigils to represent what you cut and what you keep.

to Magical Resistance

When you have your words, with a paring knife and your apple (or substitute), trace a faint line in the skin to divides the apple into two roughly equal halves from the top stem to the bottom and back again.

On one hemisphere of the apple, use the tip of the paring knife to inscribe the word you've chosen to represent your power. On the opposite hemisphere of the apple, carve the word you've chosen to represent who or what you are cutting away.

As you carve the signs or letters, reflect on what these words mean to you. More than that, reflect upon the people, experiences, and circumstances that have led you to the point where you know this toxic force in your life must be cut away. How did you become entangled? How much of your own power do you feel you have lost? What hurt and healing has happened along the way?

When you have charged the apple with all these complex feelings and intentions, set it on the cutting board and take up the larger knife. Are you ready to sever your connection? Are you hungry to make yourself whole?

Safely but decisively, chop the apple in half as close as you can along the faint line drawn to bisect it. Aim to cut so one word is completely on one cut half and the other word is completely on the other cut half.

Take a moment to feel that severing. The sharp, complete removal of this force upon your sense of self.

Take the half of the apple with the word you are removing and dispose of it. For myself, I enjoy the visceral glee of walking into my backyard and hurling that half as far as I can into the trees on the edge of my property. Everyone's circumstances are different, so you may have to dispose of your apple-half differently. Consider cleanliness and safety, the well-being of any animals living around you, but make that disposal count. Make it meaningful. Really feel it.

Then, once you have yeeted the unwanted half of the apple, speak aloud what the remaining half represents. Feel that, too. And, as you

The Gorgon's Guide

reflect on that previously surrendered piece of your power, take a bite of the remaining half of the apple. Eat as much as you can enjoy. Be present in the feel and the taste and the nourishment of the physical fruit and also what it has been magicked to represent.

Clean things up and return to your life nourished and a little more whole.

Separation and Recuperation Spell

Rev, Laura González

THE SEPARATION AND RECUPERATION SPELL is intended to be used by folks who feel that an undesired attachment remains after a breakup with other persons or situations. This is especially healing and empowering if there was emotional or physical abuse, gaslighting or disloyal behavior.

🪶 YOU'LL NEED:

¶ Tools for your craft and altar set

¶ A cauldron

¶ Matches

¶ A cup

¶ Libation

¶ An item that reminds you of the person/situation you'll be separating from (Photograph, letter, piece of clothing, etc)

PROCEDURE:

1. Cleanse your space and yourself.

2. Set up your altar and create a magic circle following your tradition.

3. Set the matches, cauldron and libation cup on the altar.

4. Bless and cleanse the item with the elements, following your tradition.

5. After you cleanse the item, hold it in your projective hand and say these or similar words:

The Gorgon's Guide

This will be the last time we are together. When you leave, I'll remain complete within and without.
Any memories of you will be a memory of me. After this moment you hurt me NO MORE!

6. Burn the item within the cauldron and say these or similar words, repeating them until the item is nothing but ashes:

   I destroy any binding that could unite us.
   I free you, I free me.
   I liberate you, I liberate me.
   I release you, I am FREE!

7. Put a pinch of the ash on your libation and say these or similar words:

   I recuperate the strength I gave you.
   I recuperate the time I gave you.
   I recuperate my dignity, it is mine forever.
   I recuperate the love I once gave you.
   It's mine and for me!

   I do this in perfect love and perfect trust. I do this in harmony with the Universe!

   So mote it be!

8. Drink the libation and sit in contemplation, letting any and all emotions run through you. Feel how what was once lost is coming back to you, and, when you feel joyful and complete, give thanks and open the circle following your tradition.

   The work is done.

Strength in Stillness
The Weavers

THE PURPOSE OF THIS RITUAL is to find strength in stillness when the world feels intense or overwhelming. Every ingredient in our herb anointing was chosen by each of our covenors for this specific ritual. May it uplift you, encourage you, and refuel you for your path ahead.

Please make sure to practice fire safety during this ritual. Have a stable surface to put your candle on, have a fire extinguisher on hand, and do not leave burning candles unattended.

PREPARATIONS

ITEMS NEEDED

- One plain candle, any size, shape, or color, preferably without a casing (jar, wrapper, ribbons, etc.). A tealight candle can work just fine if that size is what you want to use.

- A fire-safe plate or holder for the candle

- A lighter or match

- Oil to anoint the candle (we like olive oil the best)

- Dried herbs for anointing (list and instructions below)

- A playlist of songs or sounds you want to dance to, approximately 10–20 minutes long

- Food and water for grounding after the ritual

DRIED HERBS FOR CANDLE ANOINTING:

ROSEMARY for its Mediterranean roots, for strength and protection, as well as the connection to Aphrodite

Mint or Spearmint for their connections to the Underworld and to provide refreshing perspectives

Lemon Balm for its incredible resiliency

Lavender for stillness and fortification

Bay Laurel for protection from negativity and the strength to fight it

Nettle for self-nurturing and justice

CANDLE ANOINTING INSTRUCTIONS

1. Lay down some newspaper or cardboard to protect the surface you are working on.

2. If you want to carve anything into your candle (symbols, numbers, phrases, Deity names, etc.) now is the time to do so. A sewing pin works great for this.

3. Dip your fingers into the oil you've chosen and rub the candle with it. You are welcome to add essential oils to the oil base before spreading it on the candle. *Additional note: There are lots of thoughts on what direction to spread the oil for different intentions. Follow your intuition.*

4. Sprinkle the herbs onto your covered work surface and roll your candle in them. They will stick to the oil you have spread on the candle.

5. Feel free to add any additional touches. Some examples include dripping wax on top of the herbs from another candle or adding glitter for some extra sparkle. Be as creative as you'd like. Don't be afraid to get messy!

6. Let dry for 24 hours.

to Magical Resistance

THE RITUAL

If you feel called to do so, cast circle using your favorite method. You are welcome to call any guides, Deities, ancestors, or spirits that you work with into your space.

Light your anointed candle.

Take a moment to ground and center yourself. Take a few deep breaths and settle into this space.

Hit "play" on the playlist you've chosen or created. If the songs are downloaded or streaming, we recommend having your device on airplane mode so that the playlist stops with the last song.

Dance. Raise energy! It can be wild, subtle, swaying, jumping, yelling, singing, chanting, stomping, drumming, smooth, jittery, however you are feeling inspired to… move your body! Get your heart going and follow your passion! *Additional note: Feel free to adapt this for your body. You can do this sitting, standing, lying down, hands only, feet only, in your mind's eye… whatever you want to do that feels empowering and free. If your inner critic starts to speak up, invite them to tea later and return to the movement.*

Once the playlist ends, STOP. Sit. Be with the energy you raised. Soak it up. Find strength in this stillness. Feel the buzz, notice any sensations you feel in your body, and take a moment to listen. Let your magickal practice hold you. Be present with this energy as long as you wish.

Blow out the anointed candle if it hasn't gone out on its own.

If you cast circle to begin the ritual, take down circle when you are ready.

Grab a bite to eat and drink some water. Nourish. Replenish.

Rest.

> From our web to you, we wish you all the best.
> May you return to this ritual
> anytime you wish.

Acknowledgments

As with *The New Aradia*, I woke up with the need and the knowing that the time had come for the next volume. The muses and spirits don't operate on convenience or availability. Once again, Jenn Zahrt was up for the monumental task of making this book a physical reality—despite a short timeline and an equally daunting schedule. Jenn's keen eye for editing, style, concept, and format are exceptional and I'm honored that *The Gorgon's Guide's* home is Revelore Press.

We received an overwhelming number of submissions for this book. Like an obscene amount that was far beyond our expectations. I have so much gratitude and appreciation for everyone who was inspired to share their work with us. Thank you to everyone who submitted, whether selected or not. Your interest in this project and related concepts helps light the way for change. I hope that you continue to be inspired and bring forth Gorgon energy into the world.

Contributors

Alicia "Jynx" Vervain, or "The Writ Witch," is a passionate writer, poet, storyteller, and ritual dramatist, crafting language as a spiritual offering and as a means of better coming to know Spirit and Self. As a Reclaiming witch and a student of rootwork, Jynx's omnist and pantheist perspective on spirituality and life itself is grounded in the importance of Story and Myth in understanding not only who we are and who we've been, but also who we have the potential to be. As The Writ Witch, she writes custom devotional and narrative poetry and offers in-depth dream interpretations, as well as delving into bibliomancy and rhapsodomancy as personal daily practice. An avid researcher, belly dancer, full-spectrum doula, and activist for comprehensive sex education and reproductive rights, Jynx works primarily with Persephone, Inanna, the Dead, and her Self.

Brian "Chase" Charles is the illustrator of *Orphic Hymns Grimoire*. In addition to illustrating, he reads tarot, casts spells for hire, and teaches sorcerous illustration in Pittsburgh, and at festivals all over the mid-Atlantic region. You can inquire about his services at BrianCharlesArt@gmail.com

Rev. Christian Ortíz: Psychologist and priest of the Goddess. Coordinator of the Fraternity of the Goddess and founder of the Temple of Our Lady of the Night. Host of Saber Sanar Podcast and contributor to Circle Sanctuary Network Podcasts. He has collaborated in national and international events of neo-paganism and spirituality. He is currently director of Arka Books, works in therapeutic intervention and violence prevention, as well as in trauma healing. www.nuestrasenoradelanoche.org

Cory Thomas Hutcheson is the author of *New World Witchery: A Trove of North American Folk Magic* and the co-host of the podcast New World Witchery. He holds a PhD in American Studies from Penn State and works primarily in folklore studies, with an emphasis on North American folk magical traditions.

The Gorgon's Guide

Dodie Graham McKay is a writer, green witch, Gardnerian priestess, and filmmaker. She is inspired to document and share stories that capture the beauty of nature and the visible and invisible realms of magic and witchcraft. She is the author of the book *Earth Magic: The Elements of Witchcraft* (Llewellyn, 2021) and her documentary films include *The Winni Pagans* and *Starry Nights* (featuring Kerr Cuhulain). Dodie spends her spare time walking her dogs and facilitating a busy coven. She lives in Treaty One Territory, Homeland of the Métis Nation, Winnipeg, Manitoba, Canada. Visit her at www.dodiegrahammckay.com.

Emiliano Russo has a degree in English language, culture and translation and is a theater director graduated from the National Academy of Dramatic Arts. Since 2020 he has dedicated himself to the activity of blogger and digital creator, founding the project *L'Almanacco delle Streghe,* a portal that quickly became a reference point for many Italian witches. He is an initiate of the Temple of Ara Tradition. Among his teachers are Phyllis Curott, the Priestly Group of the Temple of Ara Italy, particularly Valeria Trisoglio with whom he also delves into aspects of Core Shamanism; Sorita d'Este; Emily Carding, Laura Tempest Zakroff and others. He holds different courses of magickal and personal growth. In March 2022 he published his first book, *La Voce di una Stega* and in Fall 2022 *L'Agenda della Mela: la Magia della Luna*, a magickal journal with a note by Phyllis Curott. He is one of the columnist of *Witches Magazine,* a British quarterly written by witches for witches.

Enrique Alberto Gómez was born in Mexico. He is an associate professor of physics and astronomy with a PhD from the University of Alabama. He has been active in the violence against women movement receiving the Fannie Lou Hamer and Grimké Sisters Award from UA. In 2014, Enrique became the first Latino president of a North Carolina branch of the National Association for the Advancement of Colored People (NAACP) supporting a fusion coalition of African American, Latinx and rural White communities. He is an initiate of the Sylvan Hearth Tradition studying to become a priest in it.

Estara Sanatani (she/they) is the founding priestex of Treebridge Witchcraft. Her first public foray into protection work was as editor of the quarterly e-journal *The Guardian's Grimoires* in the early 90s. She has since contributed to various magazines and anthologies. Currently she teaches online and writes fiction under her birth name, *Julie McCord*.

Georgia van Raalte is a scholar, author and occultist. She holds a PhD in literature from the University of Surrey, where her research explored the occult novels of Dion Fortune. She is the co-founder of Temple of Our Lady of the Abyss, a temple dedicated to the Goddess Babalon. She is the author of three books exploring the mysteries of Babalon, the most recent of which being *Babalon Hymnal: Poetry from the Abyss*.

Mx *Gwynevere Kipling*, a queer sapphic creature from the edges of the Cotswolds now residing in the Northern wilds. Inspired by that which is half-hidden by dreams and bringing the death-beauty into moments of imagined reality.

Heka deAuset hails from Saginaw, Michigan. She is a BIPOC Priestess of Isis who honors her African and Ramapough Lenape roots. She is co-founder of Mid-Michgan Pagan Alliance and founder of the Mobile BLM Memorial Project. She strives to elevate other BIPOC voices in Pagan spaces. This piece was written after watching the live stream of the first Woman's March in Washington DC.

Irisanya Moon (she/they) is an author, witch, international teacher, and Reclaiming initiate who has practiced magick for 20+ years. She has written seven books (so far), including Pagan Portals (*Reclaiming Witchcraft* - 2020, *Aphrodite* - 2020, *Iris* - 2020, *Norns* - 2023), Earth Spirit (*Honoring the Wild* - 2023, *Gaia* - 2023), and *Practically Pagan: An Alternative Guide to Health & Well-being* - 2020. Irisanya cultivates spaces of self-care/devotion, divine relationship (whatever that means to you), and community service as part of her heart magick and activism. www.irisanyamoon.com

Ivy Senna, born and raised in Thailand, is an astrolater and a practitioner of the occult. Much of herpractice is influenced by the animism of her cultural upbringing. Likewise, her interests in the esoteric are hungry and sweeping: from the Greek Magical Papyri to verbal charms to Vedic religion,

The Gorgon's Guide

Ivy is always eager to learn. She currently runs a blog at uponthealtar.com and can be found active on Instagram at @ivy.crowned

Jessica Della Janare (she / her / hers) is queer fat femme witch, poet, and professional tarot reader settled on the stolen land of the Coast Salish and Duwamish peoples. A longtime organizer and teacher with the now defunct Free Cascadia Witchcamp, you can her find her exploring Southern Italian folk practices on Instagram @inboccaallupotarot.

Joey Morris, a Celtic Creatrix and UK based daughter of The Morrigan, works very closely with tree magick and spends a lot of time communing and foraging within the spiritual ecosystem. This connection allows Joey to practise voice witchery and conduit for the Otherworld. Joey runs Starryeyedsupplies, an online Spiritual store, a Witchy Patreon, and is a self-published author as well as a contributing author to many Girl God anthologies, including *In Defiance of Oppression: The Legacy of Boudicca* (2021).

K.A.H. received her BA from Bellarmine University and MA from the University of Louisville for English Literature. From the latter she received her PhD in Humanities with a special concentration in interdisciplinary art history; in particular, her focus was postmodern spectacle. She has taught a variety of courses ranging from first year composition to special topics in humanities. Since 2007, K.A.H. has exhibited her work in numerous group and solo shows. Currently she is working with acrylic, colored pencil, watercolor, and graphite. She identifies as Gen X and Ace.

Rev. Laura González offers her intuitive gifts as Spiritual & Community Healer, Priestess, and Minister. She is a practitioner of Traditional Mexican Folk Magic, Native Philosophies, and Paganism in the Goddess tradition. As an extension of her spirituality, she is an advocate for Pagan & LGBTQIA communities, women's rights, suicide prevention, and diversity inclusion. Laura has presented workshops at numerous events, including Parliament of the World's Religions, Circle Sanctuary, and PSG. She is a volunteer ESL teacher at Aquinas Literacy Center, a gifted Tarot reader, and a podcaster and producer of Lunatic Mondays and Paganos del Mundo on CSNP.

to Magical Resistance

Laura Tempest Zakroff is a professional artist, author, performer, and Modern Traditional Witch based in New England. She holds a BFA from The Rhode Island School of Design and her artwork has received awards and honors worldwide. Laura is the author of several best-selling books and decks including *Anatomy of a Witch*, *Weave the Liminal*, *Sigil Witchery*, *Visual Alchemy*, and *The Liminal Spirits Oracle*. Laura edited *The New Aradia: A Witch's Handbook to Magical Resistance*. She helps facilitate social change at the grassroot level through wearearadia.org, a movement focused on magical resistance and education. www.LauraTempestZakroff.com

Lex Ritchie (they/them) is a trans, disabled, and neurodivergent mystic. They facilitate liminal experiences and use folk magic, spirit work, and tarot to help spiritual rebels, academic witches, and mystical revolutionaries go beyond the conventional, learn to trust their own intuition, and make their own path through the magical realm. They have a particular interest in ancestor work because they believe it is a necessary part of betraying, attacking, and dismantling whiteness, as well as a tool for learning to imagine and create a world beyond capitalism. Lex can be found online at thelexritchie.com, and on IG & Twitter @thelexritchie.

Lindsey Pszwaro is an astrologer and herbalist, combining astrology with plant medicine and human development. She is a former Waldorf educator and mother of two. Lindsey has a background in anthropology, primatology, herbal medicine, women's health, child development, depth psychology, mythology, poetry, and dream work. Lindsey is currently living primitively in a seasonal cabin in Vermont, gardening, foraging and tapping into ancient wisdom through the land. She holds client sessions, reading natal charts, forest schools her children, and holds New Moon and Full Moon ceremonies. You can find her on Instagram @lindseypszwaro or through her website: www.lindseypszwaroastrology.com

M. Belanger (he/she/they) is a Pagan author, singer, game designer, and television personality who has worked with HBO, CNN, Nox Arcana, Wizards of the Coast, Marvel AR, and Osbourne Media. A vocal advocate for the LGBTQIA+ community, Belanger is one of the few openly intersex people visible in US television. Founder of House Kheperu (1996-present),

Belanger continues to write and teach about magick, energy work, and psychic development. More at michellebelanger.com

Nova Pax Thrasher is a queer poet and witch, currently utilizing their bardic skills to pursue a Bachelor's Degree in Creative Writing and Pop Culture at The Ohio State University. A devotee of Persephone long before converting, they have been studying the religious and praxis aspects of witchcraft for 6+ years. They have a loving husband, rambunctious kitty, and elderly doggo, filling their social life with pop-punk concerts, Pokémon, and all things Marvel. When engaging in their passion, their works deal with identity, mental health, spirituality, and grief, some of which have been published by Ink&Nebula and Sonder Midwest.

Rev. Dr. P. Sufenas Virius Lupus (e/em/eir/eirs/emself) is a metagender person who has been a devoted polytheist for 30+ years, and has a 21+ year relationship with Antinous (and one of the founders of modern organized Antinoan devotion), a divine marriage to Thetis, divine fosterage to the Tetrad++, and devotions to many other Deities and Hero/ines using a queer syncretistic reconstructionist methodology. E is a fili (poet/scholar) in the Irish tradition of Gentlidecht, and has published many books, short fiction pieces, poems, and essays/articles. http://psufenasviriuslupus.wordpress.com

Philip Kane is a writer, storyteller and artist living in the south-eastern corner of England. As a member of the London Bisexual Group in the mid-1980s, he was co-editor of the first magazine for bisexuals in the UK, *The Bi-Monthly*; and in 1984 he initiated the "Politics of Bisexuality" conference that subsequently evolved into the annual UK BiCon. Philip is also an "Old Craft" witch, a founding member of the London Surrealist Group, a revolutionary socialist, martial artist and Morris dancer. Some of his work can be found via his blog sites, https://thenl.wordpress.com/ and https://thewayfaringtree.wordpress.com/

River Enodian is trans non-binary and a polytheistic witch. They are a priestex of Apollo and Hekate as well as being a passionate devotee of Dionysos and Hermes. River is a High Priestex in Blue Star Wicca and part of the leadership team of a Boston-based Blue Star coven. Additionally, they are an initiate in Alexandrian/Chthonioi-Alexandrian Wicca. River is published as Kyrene Ariadne in an essay featured in the anthology *Wings of Flame, Coils of Light: A Devotional for Apollo* by Jonathan Souza. Their blog is at www.patreon.com/TeaAddictedWitch, and you can learn more about them at www.riverenodian.com.

Sara Mastros is the author of *The Big Book of Magical Incense* and *Orphic Hymns Grimoire*. Her newest work, *The Planetary Pentacles of Solomon, Magician King* (Weiser Books, spring 2023). In addition to writing, she teaches tarot, witchcraft, Greek & Near Eastern mythology, Pan-Levantine folk magic, and practical sorcery in Pittsburgh, online, and at festivals and conventions all over. Additionally, she's a co-owner of The Fool's Dog Tarot, a leading tarot app for Android & Apple iOS devices. You can download a free sampler app at www.FoolsDog.com, check out courses and lessons at www.WitchLessons.com, sign up for her newsletter at www.MastrosZealot.com, or follow all her witchy shenanigans on Facebook or Twitter.

Fr. Sean Wilde UE is an Indigenous author, occultist, and Witch residing in New Orleans, Louisiana, and Kitchener, Ontario. He is a Cabot Priest and member of the Aurum Solis. His spiritual and magical journey began at the age of four, and his first public speaking engagement was at the age of eleven. He has spoken internationally at conferences, festivals, and universities. Trained at university in anthropology, philosophy, and religion, his postsecondary background introduced Sean to a variety of systems of thought. Sean has been a professional psychic, ghost hunter, teacher, authored Magic Without Tools, co-authored a published training manual for a Western Magical Tradition in Ontario and advised on books about living vampires.

Sidney Eileen (ze/zir/zem) is a trans nonbinary, asexual, animistic, polytheist witch, and an artist, blogger, writer, and teacher. Ze acknowledges divinity and unique natures in not just deities, but in all manner of ephemeral and supernatural beings, spirits, living beings, and the souls that embody the physical objects and spaces around us. Zir practice is lifelong and of an intuitive nature, seeking fulfillment through mutable asymmetrical balance. Zir perspective as a witch and an artist influences everything ze does.

The Gorgon's Guide

Star Bustamonte is the news editor for *The Wild Hunt*, the director of Mystic South Conference, and co-host of the monthly BlogTalk radio show, *The 4:15* with Raina Starr.

Terrance Gamble is a Mediterranean polytheist who has been studying witchcraft since his adolescence. An initiate in the Ophic Strix Tradition founded by Oracle Hekataios, he devotes much time honoring Hekate and Dionysus, as well as studying divination. He has also studied Black Rose Witchcraft and is a California Freemason and tarot reader. Terrance is also a watercolor artist and oil painter who creates devotional pieces for the many spirits he honors in his spiritual and magical practices.

The Order of the Gorgon Shield, a group of practitioners of diverse backgrounds and geographical locations, is dedicated to defending democracy and building a healthy society. It formed in 2020 with the intention of collaboratively undertaking research and development of new magickal technologies and doing magick to accomplish our aims. We encourage others to also form small groups, develop and share new techniques and technologies to meet the challenges of our day. The members of the Order of the Gorgon Shield include: Linda Bourdet, Karen Bruhin, Ivo Dominguez Jr., Gawan MacMillan, Claire Read, Gwendolyn Reece, and Peg Wilsbach.

χαίρετε! *The Weavers* is a Hellenic inspired coven within an Alexandrian Wicca tradition. We circle in the beautiful evergreens of Washington state. We are an inclusive coven and aspire to weave a web where all are welcome as they are. We primarily work with Chthonic energy and view the seasonal wheel as a balance of both life and death. If you would like to get in touch, please shoot us an email at TheWeaversofWashington@gmail.com

Thumper Marjorie Splitfoot Forge is a Gardnerian High Priest, an initiate of the Minoan Brotherhood, a Discordian Episkopos, a manager of a fetishwear shop, a recovering alcoholic, and a notary public from Houston, TX. He is currently working on his first book.

Resources

IN ADDITION TO THE RESOURCES that were compiled for *The New Aradia*, we'd like to bring to your attention some newer publications that may be of interest to you:

Blackthorn's Protection Magic:
A Witch's Guide to Mental and Physical Self-Defense
by Amy Blackthorn, Weiser, 2022

The Altar Within: A Radical Devotional Guide to Liberate the Divine Self
by Juliet Diaz, Row House Publishing, 2022

Revolutionary Witchcraft: A Guide to Magical Activism
by Sarah Lyons, Running Press, 2019

Waking the Witch: Reflections on Women, Magic, and Power
by Pam Grossman, Gallery Books, 2019

Outside the Charmed Circle:
Exploring Gender & Sexuality in Magical Practice
by Misha Magdalene, Llewellyn, 2020

Witchcraft Activism: A Toolkit for Magical Resistance
by David Salisbury, Weiser, 2019

Becoming Dangerous:
Witchy Femmes, Queer Conjurers, and Magical Rebels
Edited by Katie West and Jasmine Elliott, Weiser, 2019

Witchcraft for Healing: Radical Self-Care for Your Mind, Body, and Spirit
by Patti Wigington, Rockridge Press, 2020

Visual Alchemy: A Witch's Guide to Sigils, Art & Magic
by Laura Tempest Zakroff, Llewellyn, 2022